The lessons in this book cover the most tested and necessary comprehension strategies and skills in Reading/English Language Arts.

Advisory Panel

Marcia Klemp, *Reading Specialist*
Linda Fund, *Reading Specialist*
Katherine Ramsaur, *Retired Teacher/Math Coordinator*
Robert Katulak, *Assistant Superintendent for Elementary Education*
JoAnn Corry, *Reading Specialist*
Laura Johnson, *Coordinator, Reading/Language Arts*
L. Ronayne, *Vice Principal*
Lois Penny, *SFA Reading Facilitator*
Theresa Flynn-Nason, *Reading Specialist*
Kimberly Fox, *Special Education Teacher*
Jane Grimes, *ELA Curriculum Coordinator*
Alice Talbot, *Reading Specialist*
Janice Jones, *Curriculum Specialist*
Rita Reimbold, *Reading Specialist*
Jan Steuerman, *Literacy Specialist*

Your partner in student success™
299 Market Street • Saddle Brook, NJ 07663
Phone: 800-822-1080 • Fax: 201-712-0045
www.PeoplesEducation.com

ISBN 978-1-4138-3678-3
1-4138-3678-X

Printed in the United States of America.

10 9 8 7 6 5 4 3 2 1

Contents

UNIT 4 Taking Flight SUMMARIZE

UNIT 5 Elephants MAKE INFERENCES

UNIT 6 Super Sports FACT AND OPINION

UNIT 7 The Great Depression CAUSE AND EFFECT

UNIT 8 Forensic Solutions PROBLEMS AND SOLUTIONS

Dear Student,

Does it ever seem to you like there are two kinds of readers? The first kind can understand just about anything without even thinking. Reading seems easy. The second kind sometimes needs to read things over again to understand them. Reading seems like hard work.

If you are already the first kind of reader, this book will teach you to be even better. Learning new ways to think about reading will make it easier to understand whatever you read, whether it's a novel, a magazine article, or a textbook.

If you're not always the first kind of reader, *don't worry!* This book will teach you keys to understanding all kinds of reading material, including **fiction, science, social studies,** and **math**. You will start to really understand what you read without even thinking about it. Before long, you can be the first kind of reader, too.

Happy Reading!

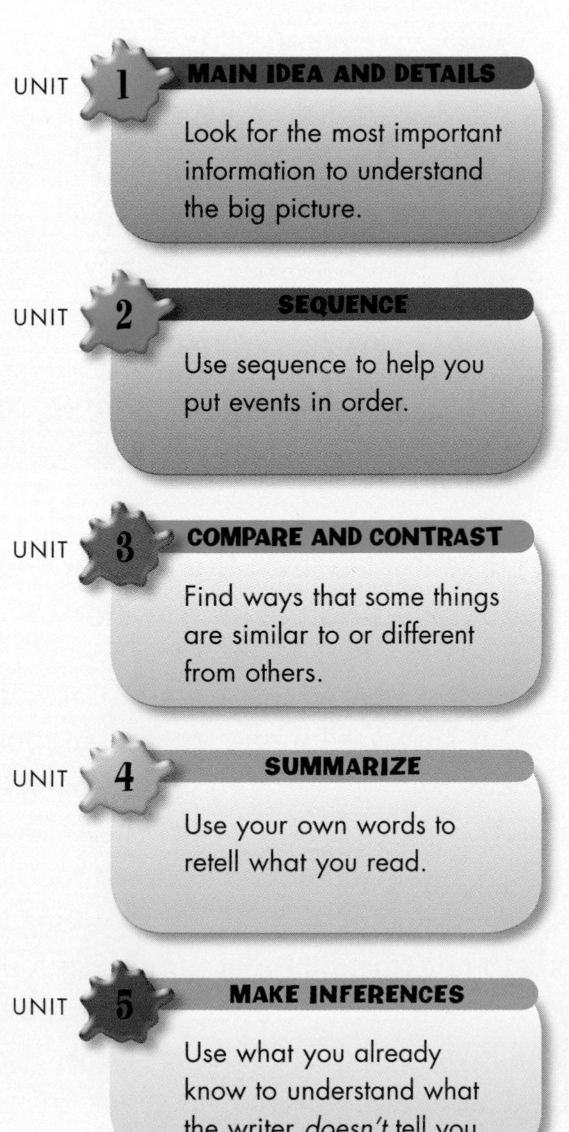

UNIT 1 **MAIN IDEA AND DETAILS**
Look for the most important information to understand the big picture.

UNIT 2 **SEQUENCE**
Use sequence to help you put events in order.

UNIT 3 **COMPARE AND CONTRAST**
Find ways that some things are similar to or different from others.

UNIT 4 **SUMMARIZE**
Use your own words to retell what you read.

UNIT 5 **MAKE INFERENCES**
Use what you already know to understand what the writer *doesn't* tell you.

UNIT 6 **FACT AND OPINION**
Look for information that can be proven true to separate facts from opinions.

UNIT 7 **CAUSE AND EFFECT**
Find out why things happen and what might happen as a result.

UNIT 8 **PROBLEMS AND SOLUTIONS**
Think about problems and how they might be solved.

Setting Foot on Antarctica

Main Idea and Details in Fiction

The **main idea** is what a story or paragraph is mostly about. Supporting **details** give more information about the main idea.

Story elements, such as characters, setting, and plot, are the main ideas that make up a fiction story. Supporting details about story elements help make the main ideas clear.

- **Main Idea:** *Jack was adventurous.*
- **Supporting Detail:** *He stowed away on a strange ship.*

Use the highlighted sentences and the Reader's Guide to identify main ideas and details in this story.

What **main idea** about Jack is found in this paragraph?

____

____

Sneaking around a busy ship in the daylight was not the easiest thing to do, but Jack was hungry. He had to move around the ship quietly. He was, after all, a stowaway. If anyone caught him, he would surely be thrown overboard.

Jack was an orphan and had landed on Deception Island after a long voyage on a whaling ship. He was looking for a better life, but that's not what he found on Deception Island. The island was hundreds of miles south of the tip of South America, and it was a terrible place to live in 1820.

Jack would have done almost anything to get off the island, and one night not long ago, he did. He stowed away on a ship in the middle of the night. The ship was called *Hero*, and Captain Nathaniel Palmer was its commander.

Jack quietly tiptoed along the deck of the *Hero*, looking for bits of food. It was November, late spring in this part of the world. At this time of year, it was light almost all day long, so it was never easy to sneak around. Just as Jack reached behind a barrel to snatch a crust of bread, he heard a voice.

"This cannot be correct, can it?" Jack recognized the voice right away—Captain Palmer. He was standing behind the ship's wheel and looking through a telescope. "My map shows no coast here, yet I see icy shores."

"Perhaps it is an undiscovered country, sir," said another voice. Jack thought it might be the first mate, but he didn't dare look. "You would go down in history if you made such a discovery," the man said.

Jack's heart raced in his chest. It wasn't from fear, but from excitement. He couldn't believe his luck. He was on a ship that was about to make a great discovery!

Suddenly, Jack was lifted off his feet and pushed against the railing by the ship's cook. "I knew there was a little rat on board stealing food," the man hissed. "Let us see how well you steal food where there isn't any."

A few rough minutes later, Jack was sitting, alone, in the *Hero's* small lifeboat. "Good luck, little rat," the cook growled, lowering the lifeboat down to the icy waters with a rope. "You'll be needing it."

Darkness came quickly, and freezing wind began to lash at the boat. Jack felt around in the boat and found a small blanket. He drifted through the darkness for what seemed like hours. Then the lifeboat struck something big, throwing Jack over backwards. Feeling around with his foot, Jack felt ice, firm ice—solid ground!

What **detail** shows that the man speaking was a ship's captain?

____

____

____

Check Your Understanding

Do you:

__ look for story elements as you read?

__ find details that support the main ideas?

Write a sentence describing the setting in the paragraph.

____

____

____

In the moonlight, Jack could barely make out icy mountains towering above him. He had reached Captain Palmer's unknown land! There was no one around, and Jack heard nothing but the sound of the wind and the waves. He scanned the dark waters and suddenly noticed a small light that looked like the glow of a faraway candle. Could it be another ship?

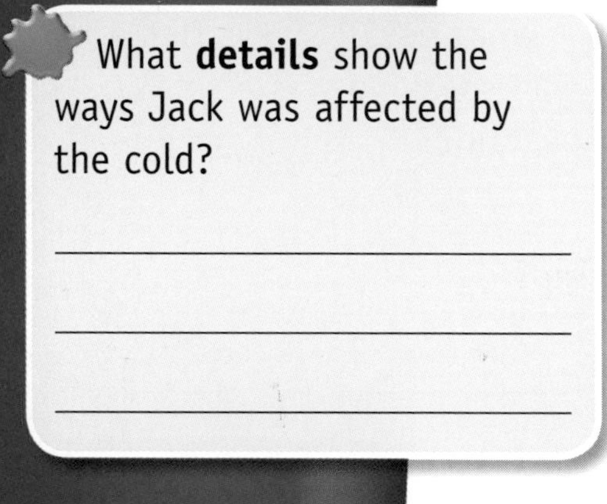

What **details** show the ways Jack was affected by the cold?

Pushing off the icy shore with his foot, Jack began to row with one of the banged-up oars in the boat. His arms began to ache, and his fingers went numb with cold, but he rowed on toward the distant light. Before he could even understand what was happening, he blacked out.

When Jack woke up, he was surprised to find himself in a warm bunk below the deck of a strange ship much bigger than the *Hero*. The strange ship had rescued him just in time. Jack got out of bed and climbed up on deck, where the morning was bright and cold. What he saw next amazed him.

Jack's old ship, the *Hero,* was anchored right next to them, and both ships looked out over a large, icy landscape—Captain Palmer's undiscovered country. Then Jack heard a familiar voice. Captain Palmer was standing on the deck of the strange ship, speaking with its bearded captain.

"We will name it Palmer Land for the man who discovered it," said the bearded captain with a thick Russian accent.

"I may have spotted this new land," Captain Palmer said, "but only time will tell who will set foot there first."

What is the **main idea** of the story's final paragraph?

Jack remembered using his foot to push the lifeboat off the icy shore. Smiling, he felt the bright sun on his face and wondered if anyone would ever know that he was the first person to set foot on Antarctica.

Keep Thinking

Think about the story "Setting Foot on Antarctica." Circle the letter next to the best answer.

1. Which **details** tell about the setting in this story?
   - A cold and windy
   - B warm and sunny
   - C dark and rainy
   - D hot and stormy

2. What caused the cook to think there was a stowaway on the ship?
   - A He found Jack hiding in the lifeboat.
   - B He had seen Jack sneak onto the ship.
   - C He talked to Captain Nathaniel Palmer.
   - D He noticed that food was missing.

3. What is the correct sequence of events in the story?
   - A Jack crept on board the *Hero*, woke up in a different ship, and then set foot on an unknown land.
   - B Jack overheard the captain, was captured by the cook, and then was stranded in a lifeboat.
   - C Jack set foot on an unknown land, crept on board the *Hero*, and then overheard the captain.
   - D Jack was stranded in a lifeboat, crept on board the *Hero*, and then set foot on an unknown land.

Write your answers on the lines.

4. What are two reasons that Jack had to sneak around very carefully on the boat?

____

____

5. Write a new title for the story that includes a clue to its **main idea**.

____

6. Use **details** from the story to describe the character of Jack.

____

____

____

Get Organized

Show the **main ideas** from the story "Setting Foot on Antarctica" by filling in the story elements below.

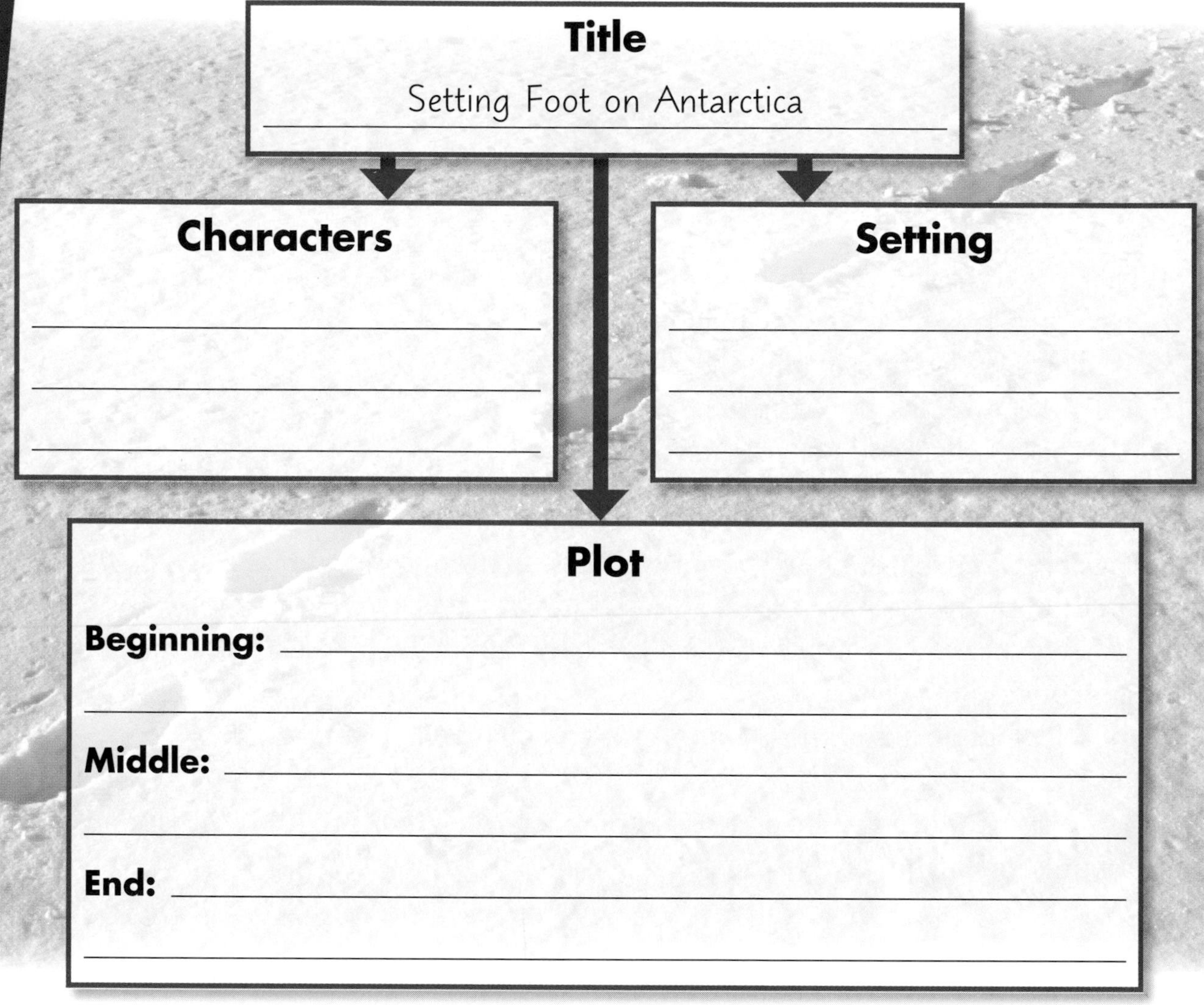

Title
Setting Foot on Antarctica
Characters
Setting
Plot
Beginning:
Middle:
End:

Summarize

Suppose that you are creating a trading card set called "Great Explorers." You want to include a card for Jack, the boy who set foot on Antarctica. Write the description for the back of Jack's card.

Write Away!

Team Up

Work with a partner. Imagine ways that the plot of this story would be different if Jack had been the captain of the *Hero* instead of a stowaway. Describe the new plot of the story below.

Beginning: ______________________________

Middle: ______________________________

End: ______________________________

On Your Own

Use the new plot you created above to write a short story about Antarctica. Include story elements as the **main ideas,** and provide supporting **details** about each one.

WRITER'S CHECKLIST

- ☐ Include story elements, such as characters, setting, and plot.
- ☐ Support each story element with details.
- ☐ Make sure your story has a clear beginning, middle, and end.

Welcome to Antarctica

Main Idea and Details in Science

Science articles have many **main ideas** that are supported by **details.** Each section of a science article often has a heading, which tells the main idea of the section. Detail sentences tell more about the main idea.

- **Heading:** *A Land of Ice*
- **Main Idea:** *Ice covers most of Antarctica.*

Reader's Guide

Use the highlighted sentences and the Reader's Guide to identify main ideas and details in this article.

What is the **main idea** of the highlighted paragraph?

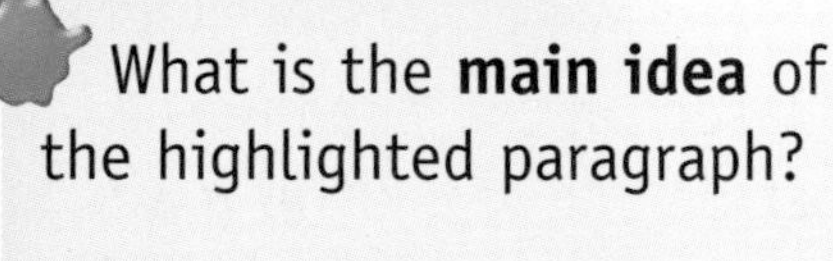

Imagine that you are visiting a research station on the continent of Antarctica. As you step off the plane or ship, the snow and ice stretch out in all directions. The air is clear and freezing cold. After all, Antarctica is one of the coldest places on Earth.

Winters in Antarctica are dark and bitterly cold. Very little sunlight reaches Antarctica between April and September. In fact, on some days the sun doesn't rise at all. During these dark winter months, the temperatures can drop to –70°F. From November to February, however, the sun shines for many hours each day. Some days even have 24 hours of sunlight. Although still cold, temperatures warm up to around 32°F.

A Land of Ice

A permanent sheet of ice covers 98 percent of Antarctica. Scientists think the ice sheet formed millions of years ago during the Ice Age. Today, the ice sheet doesn't melt much, even in the summer. A few areas of exposed rock can be found on the tops of mountains, in dry valleys, and in some places along the coast.

The ice on Antarctica seems solid, but it is actually in constant motion. Ice flows slowly down the mountains as **glaciers**. Some glaciers feed into immense ice shelves, thick areas of floating ice attached to the continent. Sometimes, ice breaks off from the ice sheet to form icebergs. Some icebergs can be as large as a small country!

In winter, the surface of the ocean around the ice shelves freezes, too. The freezing and melting of the sea ice causes the size of the continent to grow and shrink with the seasons. Strong winds and currents wear away the ice, creating unusual points and arches.

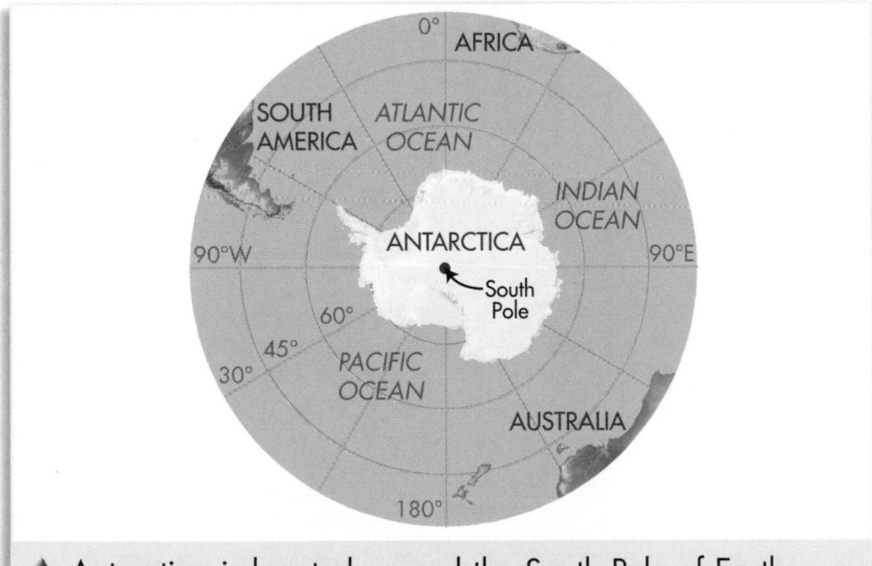

▲ Antarctica is located around the South Pole of Earth.

Can Plants Survive?

Although most of Antarctica is covered with snow and ice, a few plants live in rocky, exposed areas. Most of the continent is actually considered a desert, since very little rain or snow falls each year. Plant life must deal with a lack of moisture, low temperatures, and long periods of darkness. As a result, most plants are small and slow-growing. These plants include mosses, algae, and a combination of algae and fungus known as **lichen**.

glaciers large, slow-moving rivers of ice

What **detail** supports the **main idea** that the ice is in motion?

____

____

____

Check Your Understanding

Do you:

_ use headings to help find main ideas?

_ look for details that explain main ideas?

Based on the heading, what do you think the **main idea** of this section will be?

____

____

____

lichen algae and fungus growing together as one plant

What is the **main idea** of the highlighted paragraph?

____

____

____

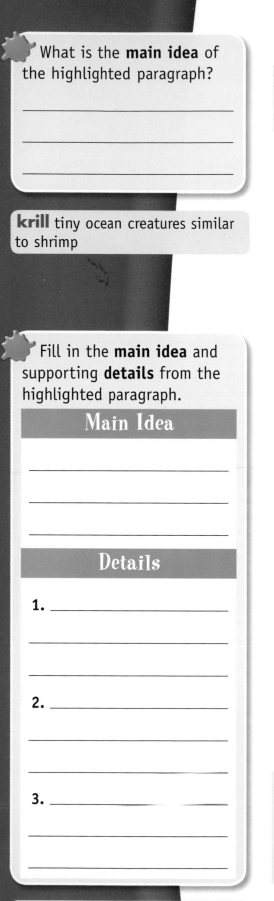

krill tiny ocean creatures similar to shrimp

Fill in the **main idea** and supporting **details** from the highlighted paragraph.

Main Idea

____

____

____

Details

1. ______________________________

____

____

2. ______________________________

____

____

3. ______________________________

____

____

ecosystem the living and non-living things in a single place

Paradise for Penguins

Many animals live on the continent of Antarctica and its nearby islands. With so few plants there, the animals of Antarctica depend on the ocean for survival. The ocean provides food for many species of whales, seals, and penguins.

Penguins are birds that eat small fish and **krill** from the ocean. They cannot fly, but they are fast swimmers. They steer with their short tails and feet. To survive in the icy water, penguins have outer feathers that overlap to keep water out. They also have a thick layer of soft feathers called down next to their skin to keep warmth in. Penguins are so well adapted to the cold that, on a sunny day, they can become overheated.

At 40 to 50 inches tall, emperor penguins are the largest penguins anywhere in the world. They live in colonies on the Antarctic ice. Emperor penguins dive in the ocean for food. They have the longest and deepest dives of any bird, diving as deep as 1,700 feet for up to 20 minutes at a time.

▲ Emperor penguins live in colonies on the icy land.

Emperor penguins cope with the Antarctic climate in interesting ways. The female penguin lays her egg during the winter, and the male penguin holds the egg on his feet, keeping it warm under a flap of skin. Groups of male penguins tending eggs huddle together through harsh winter storms.

Antarctica is a vast, ice-covered continent. It's also a vibrant **ecosystem**. The changing ice and unusual plants and animals make it an interesting place to visit and study.

Keep Thinking

Think about the article "Welcome to Antarctica." Circle the letter next to the best answer.

1. What is the **main idea** of the article?
- **A** The ice on Antarctica is constantly moving.
- **B** Few plants can survive on Antarctica.
- **C** Antarctica is a unique ecosystem.
- **D** Animals of Antarctica depend on the ocean.

2. Why do you think it's difficult for people to visit Antarctica during the winter?
- **A** The sea ice and darkness make it hard to reach Antarctica.
- **B** There are no penguins living on Antarctica in the winter.
- **C** During the winter, the continent is considered a desert.
- **D** The sunshine and warm temperatures make it difficult to travel.

3. How are penguins similar to other birds?
- **A** Both penguins and other birds build nests in trees.
- **B** Penguins and all other birds are good swimmers.
- **C** Penguins and all other birds can't fly.
- **D** Both penguins and other birds have feathers.

Write your answers on the lines.

4. Why is the first heading "A Land of Ice"?

____

____

5. Write one **detail** that supports the **main idea** that penguins are well adapted to living on the continent of Antarctica.

____

____

____

6. Write two possible headings for the section "Paradise for Penguins."

____

____

Get Organized

Reread the section "A Land of Ice." Fill in the graphic organizer to show **main ideas** and **details** from that section.

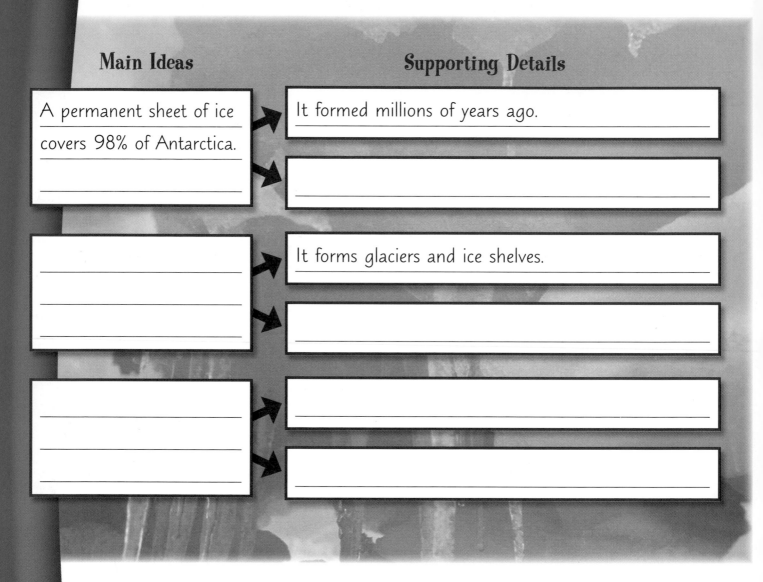

Main Ideas	Supporting Details
A permanent sheet of ice covers 98% of Antarctica.	It formed millions of years ago.
	It forms glaciers and ice shelves.

Summarize

Imagine that you are designing a Web site about Antarctica. Write the **main ideas** that you will include on your Web site.

Write Away!

Team Up

Work with a partner. Imagine that you are planning to travel to Antarctica in November. What things would you need to bring with you? List these **details** below.

1. ______________________
2. ______________________
3. ______________________
4. ______________________
5. ______________________
6. ______________________

On Your Own

Imagine that you are part of a research team on Antarctica. Think about the things that you might learn. Write a letter to a friend with **main ideas** and **details** about the weather, plants, and animals.

WRITER'S CHECKLIST

- ☐ Write a friendly letter.
- ☐ Include main ideas about the weather, plants, and animals of Antarctica.
- ☐ Include supporting details to make your main ideas more clear.

LESSON 3

DISCOVERING ANTARCTICA

Main Idea and Details in Social Studies

The **main ideas** in a social studies article are the most important facts. The **details** support the main ideas. Readers can use the main ideas and details to make a generalization, or a broad statement, about something.

- **Main Idea:** *In 1892, Antarctica became a land of important discoveries.*
- **Detail:** *Explorers made a shocking find.*
- **Generalization:** *The discovery must have been important and unexpected.*

Reader's Guide

What does the highlighted paragraph suggest the **main idea** of this article will be?

____

____

frigid extremely cold

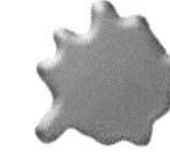

Use the highlighted sentences and the Reader's Guide to identify main ideas and details in this article.

In the early 1800s, it seemed that every place on Earth had already been discovered. Explorers longed to discover a new land. At last, they found Antarctica.

This ice-covered continent had no people and only a few animals. Why explore such a wasteland? Little did the earliest explorers know, Antarctica would turn out to be a very important discovery.

Early Exploration

For many years, the islands just north of Antarctica were known well by seal and whale hunters. None of them traveled farther south, however, because they didn't want to risk getting stuck in the **frigid**, icy seas.

In 1820, a 19-year-old sea captain from the United States named Nathaniel Palmer was sent out to find new areas to hunt seals. He saw Antarctica from his ship, but he didn't land there. Then, in 1821, another American seal hunter named John Davis did land on Antarctica, becoming the first person known to do so.

This was exciting, but no one knew exactly what to do next. The new land seemed to have no valuable resources. No one could live there because it was so icy. For the next 70 years, this newly discovered land seemed like a worthless chunk of ice.

Scientific Exploration

In 1892, however, this chunk of ice became a land of important discoveries. In that year, explorers made a shocking find. They discovered fossils on Antarctica.

Through careful study of these fossils, scientists learned that this continent had not always been buried under ice, as they had originally thought. It had once been a warm land with forests and lakes. "Antarctica fever" broke out in Europe. People wanted to find out what other surprises it held.

Early scientists had to work in harsh conditions to study Antarctica. They sailed as far as they could until their ships got trapped in sea ice. Many worked from their ships or built small huts on the ice. They traveled by dogsled to **survey** the icy land and study the fossils and climate. When the Antarctic summer came, and the ice around their ships melted, they sailed back home with their finds.

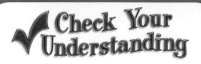

Check Your Understanding

Do you:

__ think about the main idea of each paragraph?

__ look for details that support the main ideas?

Underline the **main idea** of the highlighted paragraph.

What is one generalization you can make from the highlighted sentences?

____

____

____

survey to measure and map a piece of land

▲ Early explorers traveled by dogsled to study Antarctica.

What generalization can you make from the highlighted **details**?

treaty a formal agreement between two or more nations

Fill in the **main idea** and supporting **details** from the highlighted paragraph.

Main Idea

Supporting Details

1.

2.

These early scientists were not famous. The world was far more excited about who would reach the South Pole first, not who made the best fossil discoveries. People wondered: which nation would be the first to plant its flag at the South Pole of Earth? In 1911, the Norwegian explorer Roald Amundsen and his team won the race. Traveling by dogsled, they were the first to reach the South Pole.

This international competition was exciting, but brought some problems along with it. By the 1940s, some countries were claiming parts of Antarctica for themselves. Scientists worried that if one nation claimed a part of Antarctica for itself, it might refuse to let scientists from other nations study there.

As a result, an agreement was reached known as the Antarctic Treaty. The **treaty** said that Antarctica did not belong to any country. It was a shared space that could only be used for peaceful, scientific purposes.

Antarctica Today

Today, there are about 50 scientific research bases on Antarctica. As many as 3,000 scientists can be found there during the summer months. Most scientists work for only a few months at a time, but some stay for an entire year.

Researchers now travel on ice-breaking ships, airplanes with skis for landing, and snowmobiles. Even though technology has changed since the first Antarctic explorers set sail, the goal of the scientists there has not. They still seek to understand the wonders of this icy continent.

▲ Scientists work at Antarctic research bases like this one.

Keep Thinking

Think about the article "Discovering Antarctica." Circle the letter next to the best answer.

1. What is the **main idea** about Antarctica presented in the article?
- **A** Antarctica is a challenging but worthwhile place to study.
- **B** Researchers have to get to Antarctica in unusual ways.
- **C** Reaching the South Pole was more exciting than doing research.
- **D** At first, people thought Antarctica was a wasteland.

2. Why was Antarctica a disappointing discovery at first, compared to other new lands?
- **A** It didn't have any new areas for seal or whale hunting.
- **B** It was too far away for countries to claim for their own.
- **C** No one could live there, and it had no natural resources.
- **D** No one could land on it because of the surrounding sea ice.

3. What happened right *before* "Antarctica fever" broke out in Europe?
- **A** Researchers realized Antarctica might melt.
- **B** Roald Amundsen won the race to the South Pole.
- **C** The race to the South Pole began.
- **D** Fossils were discovered on Antarctica.

Write your answers on the lines.

4. What was the job of the first people to see and land on Antarctica?

____

____

5. In the article, what **details** support the following **main idea**?

Early scientists had to work in harsh conditions to study Antarctica.

____

____

____

6. How does the Antarctic Treaty help scientists from all nations?

____

____

Get Organized

Complete the web below. Write four **details** that support this **main idea** about Antarctica.

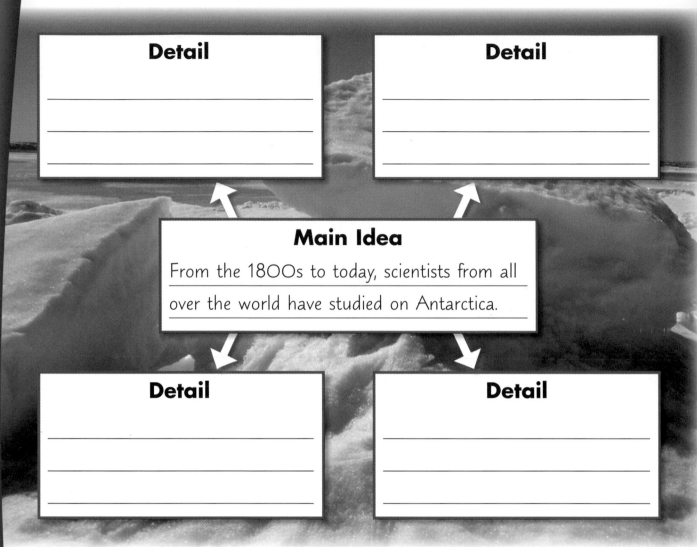

Detail

____

____

____

Detail

____

____

____

Main Idea

From the 1800s to today, scientists from all over the world have studied on Antarctica.

Detail

____

____

____

Detail

____

____

____

Summarize

Imagine that you are a reporter covering the race to the South Pole 100 years ago. Write a brief article describing why the discovery of Antarctica's wilderness is also important.

____

____

____

____

Write Away!

Team Up

Work with a partner to brainstorm ways that life at a research base on Antarctica might be similar to or different from where you live. List your ideas below.

1. ______________________________
2. ______________________________
3. ______________________________
4. ______________________________
5. ______________________________

On Your Own

Using what you've learned about Antarctica, write a paragraph about what it might be like to live on an Antarctic research base. Present your **main idea**, and then include **details** that support it.

WRITER'S CHECKLIST

- ☐ Start with a main idea about what you think base life would be like.
- ☐ Include details that support your main idea.
- ☐ Describe the challenges you might face and need to overcome.

LESSON 4

Antarctic Ice

Main Idea and Details in Math

In math, the title and headings of a chart or graph give the **main idea**. The numbers give the **details**.

A fact sheet is a type of chart that lists the most important or interesting details about a single main idea.

Gather Information **Read the fact sheet below about ice on Antarctica.**

Antarctic Ice: A Fact Sheet
• Antarctica contains 90% of all the ice on Earth.
• Antarctica has an area of 5.4 million square miles, larger than the United States.
• 98% of Antarctica is covered by ice.
• The average thickness of the ice is 1.5 miles.
• The thickest ice is almost 3 miles thick.
• In winter, the sea ice around Antarctica grows at a rate of 40,000 square miles per day.
• The area of sea ice around Antarctica grows from 1.2 million square miles in summer to 7.7 million square miles in winter.

Understand a Bar Graph

A bar graph lets readers compare different amounts. The graph below compares the thickness of Antarctic ice in different places. Use the graph and the fact sheet to answer the questions.

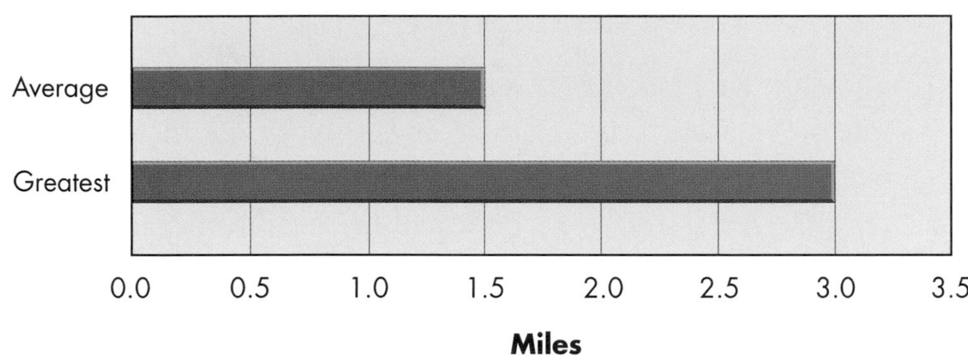

1. What is the **main idea** of the fact sheet? Of the bar graph?

____

____

2. What is the difference (in miles) between the thickest part of the ice and a place of average thickness?

____

3. How much greater is the area of sea ice in the winter than in the summer?

____

Make Your Own Bar Graph

Complete the bar graph below to compare the area of sea ice around Antarctica in summer and winter. Use information from the fact sheet to draw the missing bars.

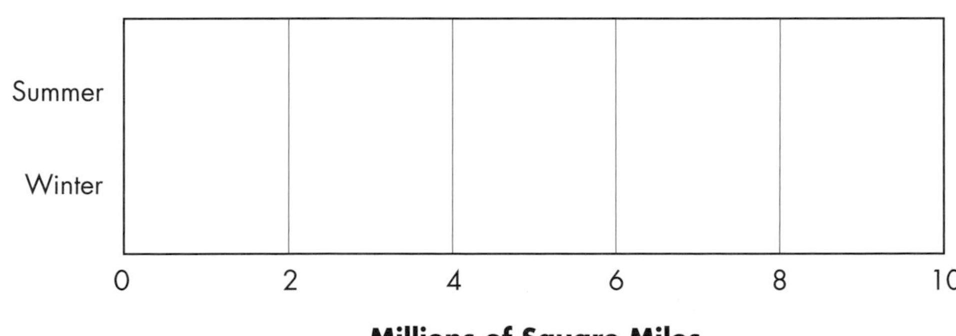

Making Connections

Read the article below. Then answer the questions.

Ice Swimming

In 2002, Lynne Cox was the first person ever to swim to the shore of Antarctica. Cox had tackled many other swimming challenges in the past, but the Antarctic swim would be her greatest adventure.

Water in the ocean around Antarctica is extremely cold, almost freezing. It can cause a person to lose body heat quickly. Breathing and heart rate can slow down to dangerous levels. Luckily, Cox had practiced swimming in very cold water since she was young.

Cox was in great shape for the swim, but she also needed to be prepared for other challenges. Animals of Antarctica, such as Orca whales, can be dangerous. There are also huge waves and sharp chunks of ice in the water.

Lynne Cox spent several years preparing for her Antarctic swim. She ate a special diet to raise the amount of fat in her body to act as insulation against the cold water. She also grew her hair long. She piled it on top of her head under her swim cap to keep her head warm. She used special earplugs so the frigid water could not damage her ears or brain.

The actual swim was just as challenging as Cox had expected. Drifting blocks of ice almost knocked her unconscious. Strong currents pulled her off course. Yet in the end, Cox reached her destination. She had overcome all obstacles and fulfilled her dream of swimming to the icy land of Antarctica.

1. Why is it dangerous for humans to swim in freezing-cold water?

____

2. Name one way Lynne Cox prepared for her swim to Antarctica.

____

____

3. What is the **main idea** of the article?

____

____

Apply Your Knowledge

Think about the story "Setting Foot on Antarctica" and the articles you have read in this unit. Answer the questions below.

Imagine that you are taking a voyage to Antarctica. What would you want to see most and why?

____

____

Describe three things that you would want to do during your trip to Antarctica. Write your answers in complete sentences below.

1. ____

____

2. ____

____

3. ____

____

Choose a Team Project

Choose one of the following group activities, and complete it using your knowledge of Antarctica.

Build a Boat

Work with your group to design a special boat that is meant just for trips to the cold Antarctic environment. How would the boat help people face the cold weather, icy waters, and curious animals in this part of the world? Draw plans for your boat, label all the different parts, and write a description telling what each part does. Present your plans to the class.

Travel Brochure

With your group, create a travel brochure that persuades tourists to visit Antarctica. To make your brochure, fold a sheet of paper into thirds. Divide the brochure into sections with headings. Add small drawings or photos of Antarctica. Then write about the details that make Antarctica different from any other place on Earth. Share your brochure with the class.

LESSON 5

Hana's New Home

Sequence in Fiction

Sequence is the order in which events happen. In most stories, events happen in time order, one after another.

A flashback can be used to describe an event that happened before the actual story. A flashback can tell more about a character or help readers better understand the events in the story.

Reader's Guide

When did Hana *first* hear the sound of the oud?

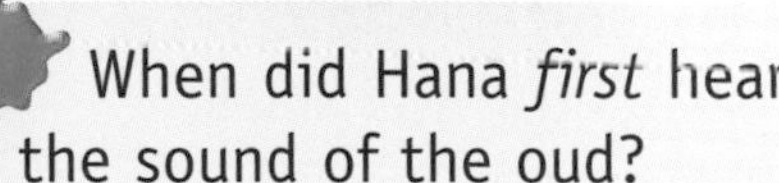

Use the highlighted sentences and the Reader's Guide to understand the sequence in this story.

Hana stopped playing the instrument and let the vibration of the strings pass through her hands, across her wrists, along her arms, and into her body. It spread through her like a chill—she loved that feeling. Then she began another song, plucking the strings and tapping her foot.

Playing always made Hana think back to the first time she had ever heard the haunting sound of the oud (OOD), an Arabic guitar. It was many years ago, when she was a small child in Lebanon and had gone to visit her grandparents. The moment Hana had walked into their house, the beautiful sound of the oud enchanted her.

She followed it down the hallway to a room where her grandfather sat on a stool playing the instrument. He swayed gently to the rhythm, eyes closed, plucking the strings with a trimmed eagle's feather. Instantly, Hana wanted to know how to make that sound, and she asked her grandfather to show her how.

Hana, along with her parents and her brother, had left Lebanon and moved to Virginia three months ago. In the time since they had immigrated to the United States, life had seemed very strange. Their old house in Lebanon had always been filled with friends, family, and music. Now the only thing Hana had left to remind her of those times was the oud her grandfather had given her before she left.

When had Hana's family immigrated to the U.S.?

____

On her first day of school, before her math class started, an interesting student entered the room and sat at the desk beside Hana's. The boy had black, twisted hair, and he wore a leather jacket with weird designs painted on it. Next to his desk was a large guitar case covered with stickers. Hana stared at the guitar case. She couldn't help it. Every time she saw anything even close to an oud, her fingers itched to play it.

What were the *first* two things Hana noticed about the boy?

1. ______________________

____

2. ______________________

____

"Hi, I'm Danny," the boy said, leaning over.

"I'm Hana," she said, feeling embarrassed for staring.

Danny noticed Hana staring at his guitar. "Do you play?" he asked, and before she could answer, he grabbed the guitar out of its case and handed it to Hana.

Smiling, Hana set the guitar on her lap and plucked a single note. It rang perfectly clear and felt wonderful. "I play the oud," she said, handing the guitar back to Danny.

"What's an oud?" Danny asked.

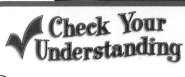

Check Your Understanding

Do you:

__ look for flashbacks in the story?

__ find words that show sequence?

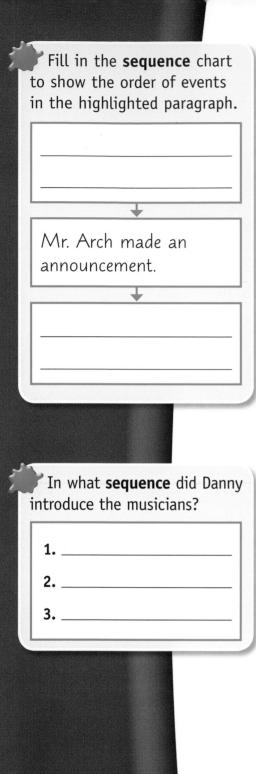

Fill in the **sequence** chart to show the order of events in the highlighted paragraph.

____________ ____________
↓
Mr. Arch made an announcement.
↓
____________ ____________

In what **sequence** did Danny introduce the musicians?

1. ____________
2. ____________
3. ____________

"It's like a guitar," Hana said, "but a little different. I learned it back in Lebanon. My family just moved here."

"That's cool," Danny said. "I moved here, too, only from Cleveland." Then his eyes lit up with an idea. "Hey, would you want to come to a jam session this Thursday after school? I have some musician friends, and we get together once a week."

"Okay," said Hana, thinking that it might be nice to meet some new friends.

Just then Mr. Arch, the math teacher, walked into the room. "Good morning, class," he announced. "For you new students, let me welcome you to McKinley Middle School. For those of you returning, please remember to put all of your belongings in your lockers before class. If I recall, we use calculators in math class, not guitars." Danny grinned at Hana, and she laughed.

On Thursday after school, Hana arrived at Danny's garage carrying her oud in its old, beat-up case. While Hana unpacked her instrument and started to tune it, Danny introduced her to the group. "This is Jordan, our amazing drummer. Over there is Ben, the best bass player around. Last but not least is Shan, who plays a mean dizi. It's a bamboo flute, and it has a totally unique sound. Shan moved here from Hong Kong last year."

"All right, everybody!" Danny shouted above the noise, "Say hi to Hana. She plays the oud."

Hana lifted her hand and waved at all the welcoming faces.

"What the heck is an oud?" asked Jordan, pointing toward Hana's instrument with a drumstick.

"Listen," Hana said, and she began to play, feeling at home at last.

Keep Thinking

Think about the story "Hana's New Home." Circle the letter next to the best answer.

1. At the end of the story, Hana *finally* felt
A that she was at home.
B like going back to Lebanon.
C embarrassed about her talent.
D ready to quit playing the oud.

2. What detail did all of the students in the story have in common?
A They all played musical instruments.
B They were all in the same math class.
C They had all come from other countries.
D They were all new students at school.

3. What effect did her grandfather's oud playing have on Hana?
A It made Hana want to move to the United States.
B Hana wanted to join a band after hearing the music.
C Hana wanted to learn how to play the oud.
D She realized that she wanted to play guitar, not the oud.

Write your answers on the lines.

4. What were Hana and Danny doing *before* math class started?

____

____

5. Number the events below 1, 2, and 3 to put them in the correct **sequence**.

______ Hana learned how to play the oud.

______ Hana started school in the United States.

______ Hana moved to Virginia.

6. Write a sentence explaining why the flashback in this story was important.

____

____

____

Get Organized

Complete the chart below to show the **sequence** of events in the story.

Hana heard her grandfather play the oud for the first time.

↓

↓

Hana attended her first day of school in Virginia.

↓

↓

Summarize

Suppose that the musical group from the story has decided to make a CD. Inside the CD case, there will be a description of the way each member came to be in the band. Write Hana's story for the CD case.

Write Away!

Team Up

Work with a partner. Imagine that you have just arrived in the United States from another country. Discuss what you would do *first, second,* and *third*.

First, ______________________________

Second, ______________________________

Third, ______________________________

On Your Own

Use your ideas from the activity above to write a story about immigrating to the United States. Write about what you would do in **sequence**, and include a flashback about the way you moved to a new country.

WRITER'S CHECKLIST

- ☐ Write a story about moving to a new country.
- ☐ Use words such as *first* and *then* to show the order of events.
- ☐ Include a flashback about the way you immigrated to the United States.

LESSON 6

Einstein: Immigrant Scientist

Sequence in Science

Writers often tell the order of events in a person's life in **sequence**. Sequence clue words, such as *before, after,* and *then,* can show the ways things changed over time.

- Einstein went to college *before* working as a clerk.
- *After* writing several science articles, he won the Nobel Prize.
- *Then* he immigrated to the United States.

Reader's Guide

Use the highlighted sentences and the Reader's Guide to understand the sequence in this article.

Which words in the highlighted paragraph help show the **sequence** of Einstein's life?

____

____

influential having a great effect

Why is the sky blue? It's a simple question. Yet no one had found the answer when Albert Einstein began his scientific career. By the age of 26, Einstein had figured out the answer to this age-old question. The sky is blue because sunlight bounces off particles in the atmosphere, reflecting all but the blue light. The blue light reaches our eyes, and we see a blue sky.

This is just one of the many discoveries Einstein made before immigrating to the United States. By that time, Einstein had become one of the most **influential** scientists in history.

Brain Child: 1879–1902

Albert Einstein was born in Ulm, Germany, in 1879. Although he was curious about science from an early age, Einstein was thought to be a slow learner. He had a difficult time in school. No one knows exactly why that was true, but some historians think that Einstein may have had a learning disability.

Despite his struggles, Einstein worked hard. He attended school and did well in math, but he was bored with many of the lessons his teachers required him to memorize. He was curious about areas of science that were not taught in school, so he read stacks of science books on his own. In this way, he taught himself what he wanted to learn.

What did Einstein do when he was bored with his lessons in school?

____

____

His Greatest Work: 1902–1933

After graduating from college in Zurich, Switzerland, Einstein wanted to be a teacher, but no schools would hire him. Instead, he took a job at the Swiss **patent** office and reviewed patents filed for inventions.

patent a government document proving ownership of an invention

In his spare time, Einstein continued to study science. He worked late into the night after long days at his clerk job. As it was later discovered, it was in these years that he developed his most important scientific theories.

When did Einstein develop his most important theories?

____

____

____

Then in 1905, at age 26, Einstein wrote five science articles that changed the field of physics. For years, scientists had been baffled by **experimental** results they could not explain. Scientists were amazed when Einstein's papers explained these results. One of his most famous works is the Theory of Relativity, which describes how matter and energy are related in the universe.

experimental based on scientific tests

▲ Einstein's early science articles changed the field of physics.

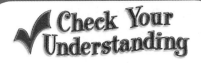

Check Your Understanding

Do you:

_ find words that show sequence?

_ look at dates to understand the sequence of events?

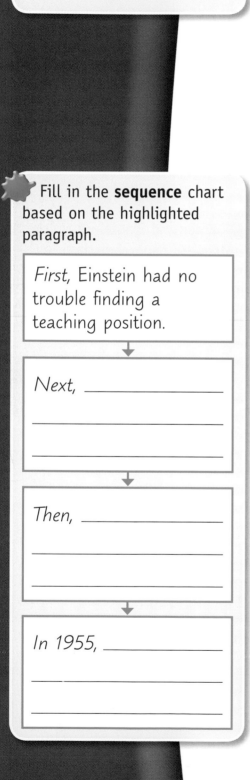

What happened many years *after* Einstein wrote his early articles?

____

____

Einstein's early science articles also changed the way that scientists explain light. Before his revolutionary ideas were published, scientists believed that light was a constant wave of energy. In 1905, Einstein proposed that light is not a constant wave, but a stream of many separate particles of energy. Based on these early papers, Einstein won the Nobel Prize in physics in 1921.

Life in the United States: 1933–1955

In 1933, when Einstein was at the height of his fame, Hitler came to power in Germany. Einstein and his wife, Elsa, decided to immigrate to the United States to escape the Nazis in Germany, who had identified the Einsteins as a Jewish family.

Since his theories were widely accepted, Einstein had no trouble finding a teaching position in the United States. He settled in Princeton, New Jersey, and continued his work in physics, always hoping to learn more about the universe. He spent the rest of his life teaching and never returned to Germany. He died in his sleep on April 18, 1955.

Albert Einstein overcame many obstacles in life to become one of the most influential scientists in history. Like many immigrants, he contributed his knowledge and culture to his new country, the United States.

Fill in the **sequence** chart based on the highlighted paragraph.

First, Einstein had no trouble finding a teaching position.

↓

Next, ______________________________

↓

Then, ______________________________

↓

In 1955, ______________________________

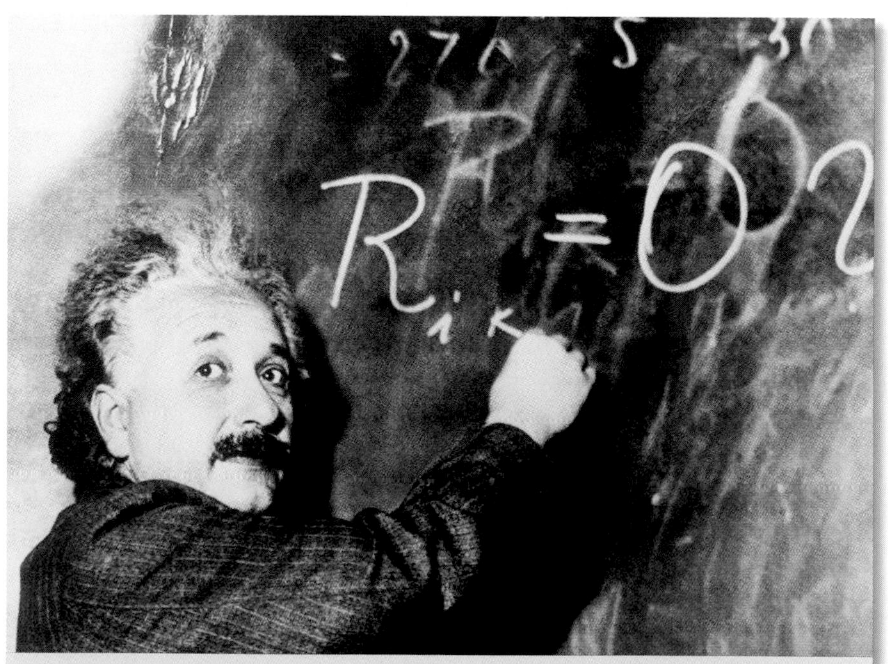

▲ Einstein spent his life teaching and learning about science.

Keep Thinking

Think about the story "Einstein: Immigrant Scientist." Circle the letter next to the best answer.

1. When did Einstein immigrate to the United States?
A in 1879
B in 1905
C in 1933
D in 1955

2. What caused Einstein and his wife, Elsa, to leave Germany?
A Einstein was fleeing the Nazis in Germany.
B Einstein had job offers in other countries.
C Einstein's theories were not widely accepted.
D Einstein's family already lived in the United States.

3. Which of the following sentences best describes the article's main idea?
A Einstein was an immigrant to the United States.
B Einstein overcame obstacles to become an important scientist.
C Einstein developed the Theory of Relativity to explain matter and energy.
D Einstein won the Nobel Prize in 1921.

Write your answers on the lines.

4. What did Einstein do *after* graduating from college?

____

____

____

5. Fill in the sentences with *Before* or *After* to describe the **sequence** of events.

______________ Einstein's ideas were accepted, it was easy for him to find a job.

______________ he moved to the U.S., Einstein won the Nobel Prize.

6. What did scientists believe about light *before* Einstein wrote his science papers?

____

____

____

Get Organized

Complete the time line below using the **sequence** of events in Einstein's life.

Summarize

Imagine that you are a news reporter in 1933. You have heard that Albert Einstein is immigrating to the United States. Write the first paragraph of the news article that describes the famous scientist.

Write Away!

Team Up

Work with a partner. Construct a time line of your own life, listing the events in **sequence**. Share your time line with your partner.

On Your Own

What challenges have you had to face in your own life? Write a short essay about your challenges and the ways you overcame them. Describe each challenge in **sequence**.

WRITER'S CHECKLIST

- ☐ Write a short essay describing challenges you have faced.
- ☐ Use sequence to put the challenges in time order.
- ☐ Explain the ways you overcame your challenges.

LESSON 7

NEW YORK: A City of Immigrants

Sequence in Social Studies

Social studies articles often describe the ways people or places changed over time. Writers explain things that happened at different times to show the **sequence** of events.

- *In the early 1600s, English settlers came to America looking for religious freedom.*
- *Today, many immigrants come to the U.S. looking for better jobs and living conditions.*

Use the highlighted sentences and the Reader's Guide to understand the sequence in this article.

In 1964, President John F. Kennedy wrote, "Everywhere, immigrants have enriched and strengthened the fabric of American life." This has been especially true of New York City. It is home to immigrants from more than 180 different countries. New York is one of the most **cosmopolitan** cities on Earth.

cosmopolitan composed of people from around the world

The United States of America has had a long history of immigration. Spanish settlers began to immigrate to America in the late 1500s. A steady stream of immigrants continued from the 1600s through the 1700s. Then larger waves of immigrants entered the country from Europe in the 1800s.

Who were the *first* immigrants to America?

____

____

Immigrants still come to the United States, and they come for a variety of reasons. Some are looking for better jobs and living conditions. Others are escaping difficult situations in their home countries. All immigrants to the United States share one thing, however, the hope of starting a new life.

Early Immigration in New York

After the Civil War ended in 1865, immigration rose sharply. New York became the first stop for millions of people seeking a better life in the United States.

In 1890, Ellis Island was chosen as the site of a new immigration station. Located in New York Harbor, it was the main port through which immigrants entered the United States. Between 1892 and 1954, about 12 million immigrants from many different **ethnic** groups passed through this port. Most of those immigrants settled in New York.

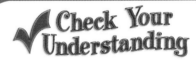

Immigration rose sharply *after* what major event?

____

ethnic from a group that shares the same country or culture

▲ From 1892 to 1954, about 12 million immigrants passed through Ellis Island.

Check Your Understanding

Do you:

_ look for dates that show sequence?

_ review headings to understand each section?

The nearby Statue of Liberty acknowledges New York's essential role in the immigrant experience. The statue represents freedom and **acceptance**. Since 1886, it has welcomed millions of immigrants to New York Harbor.

acceptance willingness to treat others as equals

When did the Statue of Liberty begin to welcome immigrants to New York?

____

A Changing City

As a result of immigration in the 1800s, New York City in 1900 had as many Irish residents as Dublin, Ireland; the largest Italian population outside of Rome, Italy; and more Jews than any other city in the world. Large groups of people from Poland, China, Lithuania, and Scandinavia also settled there.

diversity a variety of qualities

New York was drastically changed by immigration in the late 1800s and early 1900s. Immigrants brought much greater **diversity** to the city. Some people did not like the growing numbers of immigrants in their city. Others embraced these new residents. They saw the many contributions that people from other countries could make to the city.

Fill in the **sequence** chart to show where immigrants to New York have come from.

In the 1900s, ____________

Today, ____________

New York City Today

Today, there are more than 8 million people living in New York City, 2.9 million of whom were born in another country. In the early 1900s, most new immigrants came from Central, Eastern, and Southern Europe. Today, most new immigrants to New York come from Latin America and the Caribbean. The mix of nationalities created by immigration has made New York one of the most diverse cities in the world.

▲ Many immigrants eventually become U.S. citizens.

Name one way that past immigration made New York City unique.

____

This diversity has given New York City its international flavor. Walk down any street in New York and you are likely to pass restaurants serving food from every corner of the globe. You are also likely to hear people speaking in languages from all over the world.

New York City truly symbolizes what it means for the United States to be a nation of immigrants. Diverse and cosmopolitan, it is a city made great by the contributions of people from all over the world.

Keep Thinking

Think about the article "New York: A City of Immigrants." Circle the letter next to the best answer.

1. As a result of immigration in the 1800s, by 1900 New York City had
- **A** the largest Italian population outside of Rome, Italy.
- **B** the best port in the United States.
- **C** to close its doors to new immigrants.
- **D** very few people living there from other parts of the world.

2. What is the main idea of this article?
- **A** Many immigrants came to the United States after the Civil War.
- **B** New York City had as many Irish residents as Dublin, Ireland.
- **C** Today, there are many immigrants living in New York City.
- **D** New York, like the U.S. as a whole, has a long history of immigration.

3. What caused New York City to become diverse and cosmopolitan?
- **A** many international restaurants
- **B** immigrants from other countries
- **C** Spanish settlers in the late 1500s
- **D** the building of the Statue of Liberty

Write your answers on the lines.

4. During what time period was New York most changed by immigration? Explain.

____

____

____

5. When was Ellis Island important to immigration in New York City?

____

____

6. How has immigration to New York changed over time?

____

____

____

Get Organized

Use the dates in the article to complete the chart showing the **sequence** of immigration in New York City.

Summarize

Imagine that you just met a new immigrant to New York City. She would like to know the history of the city as a home to immigrants. Write the summary that you would tell her.

Write Away!

Team Up

Interview someone in your class with at least one family member who came to the United States from another country. Ask the following questions.

Who in your family immigrated to the United States? ____________________

____

Where did that person come from and when? ____________________

____

Why did he or she come to the United States? ____________________

____

On Your Own

Use the interview above to write a short essay. Describe the **sequence** of events that occurred when the person or family came to the U.S. Explain why these events were important to the

WRITER'S CHECKLIST

- ☐ Write an essay about a person or family that came to the U.S.
- ☐ Describe the sequence of events using dates or time periods.
- ☐ Explain why the events were important.

LESSON 8

Sequence in Math

In math, a **sequence** of numbers lets people track the way things change. The U.S. Census, an official tally of the population, is taken every ten years.

The Census tracks the parts of the world where U.S. immigrants were born. This information changes over time.

Immigrant Origins

Gather Information **In the year 2000, about 11% of the people living in the United States were born in other countries. The chart below shows the parts of the world where these immigrants were born.**

U.S. Immigrants by Birthplace–2000 Census

Birthplace	Number of People	Percentage of Immigrant Population
Latin America	16.0 million	52%
Asia	8.2 million	26%
Europe	4.9 million	16%
Africa	0.9 million	3%
Canada	0.8 million	2%
Australia	0.2 million	1%
TOTAL	**31.0 million**	**100%**

Understand a Pie Graph

A pie graph lets readers compare parts of a whole. The graph below presents the U.S. Census information from the chart on the previous page. Use both the chart and the pie graph to answer the questions below.

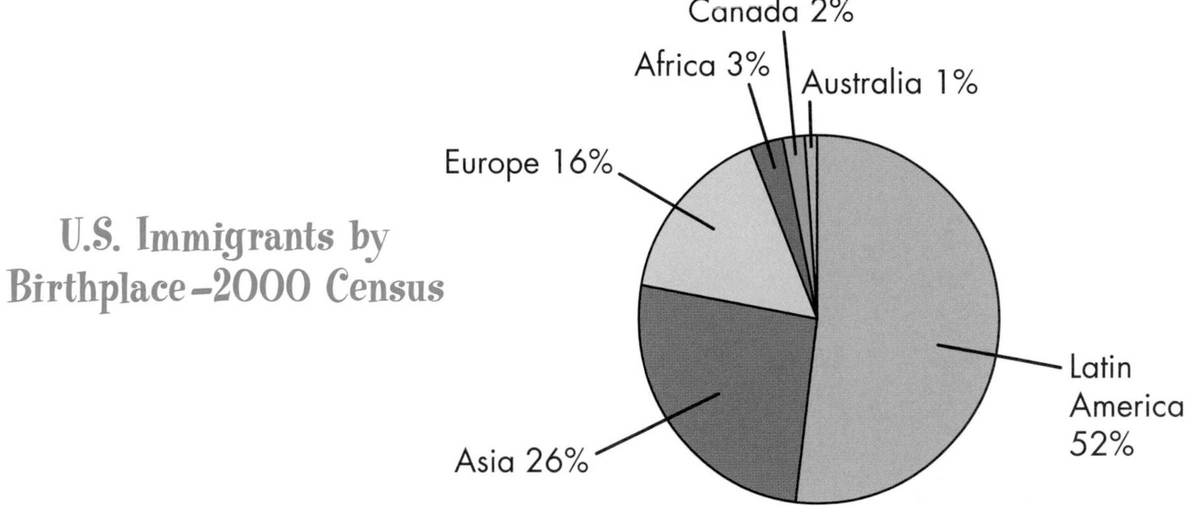

1. In 2000, what area was the birthplace of most of the immigrants living in the U.S.?

____

2. In 1990, there were 19.8 million immigrants living in the United States. How many more immigrants were living in the U.S. in 2000?

____

3. Use the totals from 1990 and 2000 to predict what the immigrant population might be in 2010.

____

____

Make Your Own Pie Graph

Use the chart below to create a pie graph that shows where people living in the United States were born.

U.S. Residents by Birthplace–2000 Census

Birthplace	Number of People	Percentage of Population
U.S.	250 million	89%
Other	31 million	11%
TOTAL	**281 million**	**100%**

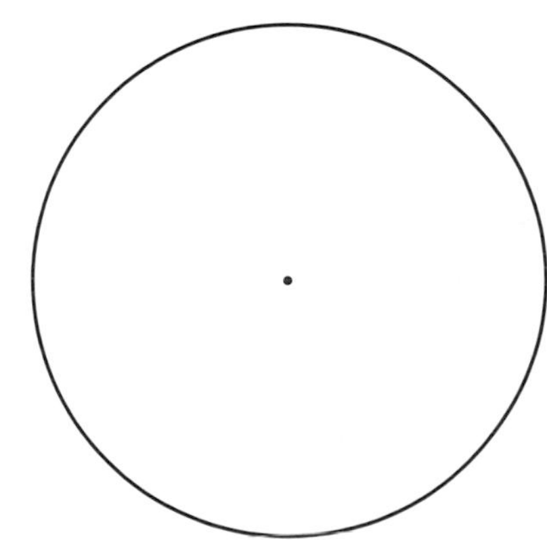

Making Connections

Read the article below. Then answer the questions.

Symbols of Freedom

"Give me your tired, your poor, your huddled masses yearning to breathe free." These poetic words appear on the base of the Statue of Liberty. The statue, representing freedom and acceptance, has welcomed millions of immigrants to the United States as they passed through New York Harbor.

The statue was dedicated in 1886. It was a gift from France, making the statue itself an immigrant to the United States. The statue was so big that it had to be taken apart and sent to the United States in boats. When it was finally put together, the statue and its base were 305 feet tall! That made it the tallest structure in all of New York.

The Statue of Liberty recognized New York's essential role in the immigrant experience. More than 12 million U.S. immigrants saw the statue on their way to nearby Ellis Island, the main port through which immigrants entered the United States during the late 1800s and early 1900s. During its peak years, Ellis Island received several thousand immigrants each day from all over the world. The port closed in 1954.

Today, the Statue of Liberty and Ellis Island are part of a national monument. They are both important symbols of the United States. Around two million people visit the monument each year. Together, these symbols serve as a reminder of the importance of immigration to the history of the United States.

1. What did immigrants see *during* their trip through New York Harbor?

____

2. What had to happen *before* the Statue of Liberty could be sent to America?

____

3. What was Ellis Island like *before* and *after* 1954?

____

____

Apply Your Knowledge **Think about the story "Hana's New Home" and the articles you have read in this unit. Answer the questions below.**

Imagine that you and your family are immigrating to a foreign country. Where would you go? How might life be different there?

____

____

____

____

If you were to move to another country, what might you miss about life in the United States?

____

____

____

____

Choose a Team Project **Choose one of the following group activities, and complete it using your knowledge of immigration.**

Family Tree

In your group, discuss the history of your family. Then draw a big family tree that shows the history of each member of your group and his or her family. Try to include as many family members as you know about. Be sure to label every person, and note whether they are immigrants to the United States. As a group, describe your family tree to the class.

A New Monument

With your group, create a new monument that represents the importance of diversity in the U.S. Draw a picture of your monument, and make a list of the steps needed to build it. Name your monument, and think of a motto for its base. Then show your monument to the class, and describe the ways that it could be an important symbol.

LESSON 9

Island Castaways

Compare and Contrast in Fiction

Writers **compare** people, places, or things in a story to show their similarities. Writers **contrast** them to show their differences.

Writers often use clue words to show comparisons or contrasts. Clue words that show comparisons include *all, both,* and *most.* Clue words that show contrasts sometimes have *–er* or *–est* endings, such as *better* or *smallest.*

- **Compare:** *The four friends were all poor sailors.*
- **Contrast:** *Mr. Holmes sailed much better than they did.*

Reader's Guide

Use the highlighted sentences and the Reader's Guide to compare and contrast in this story.

Serena adjusted the sail, but as she did, the sail swung around, and the boom almost knocked her off the boat.

"Boom!" shouted Rex, laughing as he pulled at the tangles of his mixed-up sailor's knot. "Do you get it? Boom? The pole at the bottom of the sail?"

Rex's best friend, Emilio, glanced at his sister, Marisol, and she rolled her eyes. The four friends had decided to learn to sail this summer because they were determined to find a way to get around on their own. They had grown up on the islands of the Florida Keys, but none of them had ever learned how to sail—at least not very well.

How did the sailing skills of the four friends **compare**?

____

____

"Come about!" called Mr. Holmes, the sailing teacher, who sat in the lead boat directing a trio of sailboats around a tiny island across the water. All of the sailing students began to adjust the sails to make their turns, including the four friends in the last boat. Their boat turned slowly, but the two boats ahead of them turned quickly and began to move farther and farther away.

Before the friends knew what was happening, their boat began to roll up on its side, and within seconds, it had capsized, throwing all four of them overboard. Luckily, they were near the island, and they waded through the water to the empty beach, pulling the boat behind them. The other two boats were almost out of sight.

"I can't believe it," said Serena. "We're actually ship-wrecked on a deserted island! I hope the boat is okay." She bent down to check and discovered that a knot had come loose, and one of the ropes they needed to sail the boat was gone. "Okay, now what?" she asked. The four friends sat on the beach to think.

"I'm hungry," said Rex, rubbing his stomach. "Back home there is fresh fruit in the refrigerator and a crab stand down the street. I wonder if these life vests are edible," Rex said with a silly grin.

Emilio, who was always calm in a crisis, said, "There are plenty of crabs around here. You just need to catch them. You'll find plenty of fruit, too—it's called coconut."

"What about shelter?" Serena asked. "I'm used to a roof of shingles, not a roof of palm leaves."

Contrast the way the three boats turned.

Friends' Boat

____

____

Other Two Boats

____

____

Check Your Understanding

Do you:

__ look for compare and contrast clue words?

__ think about similarities and differences?

Contrast life back home with life on this island.

Back Home

1. fresh fruit in the refrigerator
2. ______________________

On This Island

1. ______________________
2. ______________________

Circle the *-er* and *-est* words that show **contrast**.

"Complaining won't get us anywhere," Emilio said, growing very serious. "We're castaways now, and we need to start thinking like castaways," he said. "Yes, life will be tough. The sun will burn hotter, the water will be dirtier, and we might even have to eat bugs, but we have to keep our spirits up to survive. Only the smartest will make it, meaning me of course."

Then Marisol, who had been very quiet, stood up and waded into the bubbling surf before turning to face the other three. "You are all missing the big picture," she said. "Back home, we had rules—we had school, practice, and chores, but on this island, we can do whatever we want." The rest of them grew silent as they began to imagine the possibilities.

Then, suddenly, they saw a man and a woman stroll out from the palm trees carrying a red cooler. The couple was in the middle of unrolling their beach towels when they noticed the four friends staring at them.

"Who are you?" asked Rex.

"We're staying at the hotel," said the man.

"Hotel!" exclaimed Serena. "What hotel?"

The man answered by pointing toward a small sign almost hidden in the trees that said, "Beach reserved for visitors of the Castaways Resort Hotel. Swim at your own risk."

Write a sentence **contrasting** the friends' idea of the island with what it really was.

____

____

____

____

____

Emilio said, "We thought we *were* castaways, but it turns out we were just *at* the Castaways! Let's go see if the hotel has a phone we can use to call Mr. Holmes."

"And some food," said Rex. "I'm starving!"

Keep Thinking

Think about the story "Island Castaways." Circle the letter next to the best answer.

1. Who did Emilio think was smartest of the group and why?
   - A Himself, because he could handle the tough island life.
   - B Serena, because she decided to check the boat for problems.
   - C Rex, because he was always thinking about what to eat.
   - D Marisol, because she was able to see the big picture.

2. Once the friends realized they were at a hotel, what did they do next?
   - A Marisol told them to think about the big picture.
   - B They followed the two boats ahead of them.
   - C They sat down on the beach to think.
   - D They went to find a phone to call Mr. Holmes.

3. Which story detail shows that the four friends were not very good sailors?
   - A They saw a man and a woman unrolling their beach towels.
   - B They capsized the boat when they were trying to turn.
   - C They were determined to find a way to get around on their own.
   - D They had grown up on the islands of the Florida Keys.

Write your answers on the lines.

4. Write a sentence that **contrasts** the characters of Rex and Emilio.

____

____

____

5. What is one way that the couple on the beach was different from the four friends?

____

____

6. In your opinion, who had the best ideas about what to do on the island? Explain.

____

____

____

Get Organized

Fill in the diagram to **compare** and **contrast** life at home and life as island castaways.

Life at Home

1. The friends had fruit and crab to eat.
2. ______
3. ______
4. ______

Both

1. The friends could eat crab.
2. ______
3. ______

Life as Island Castaways

1. The friends would have crab and coconuts to eat.
2. ______
3. ______
4. ______

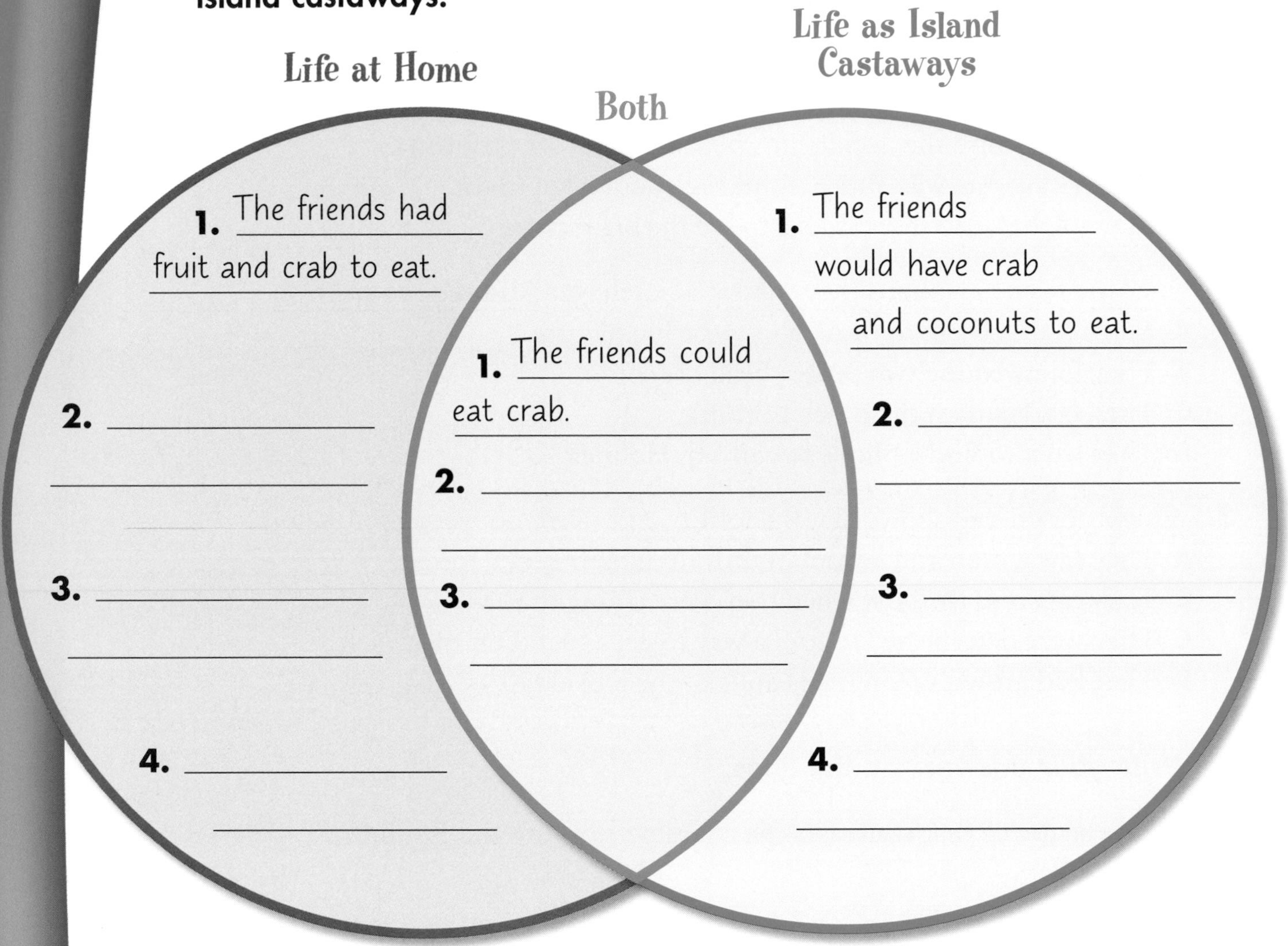

Summarize

Imagine that you are one of the friends in the story, and you have to explain to Mr. Holmes what happened. Write what you would say to him over the phone.

______

______

______

______

______

Write Away!

Team Up

Work with a partner. Make a list of three things you would each do if you were castaways on a deserted island.

My List	My Partner's List
1. ______	1. ______
2. ______	2. ______
3. ______	3. ______

On Your Own

Suppose that you were stranded on a deserted island. Write an essay that **compares** and **contrasts** your life now with life as an island castaway.

WRITER'S CHECKLIST

- ☐ Describe your life on a deserted island.
- ☐ Compare and contrast your old and new lives.
- ☐ Include at least two similarities and two differences.
- ☐ Use clue words to show comparisons and contrasts.

LESSON 10

The Galapagos Islands

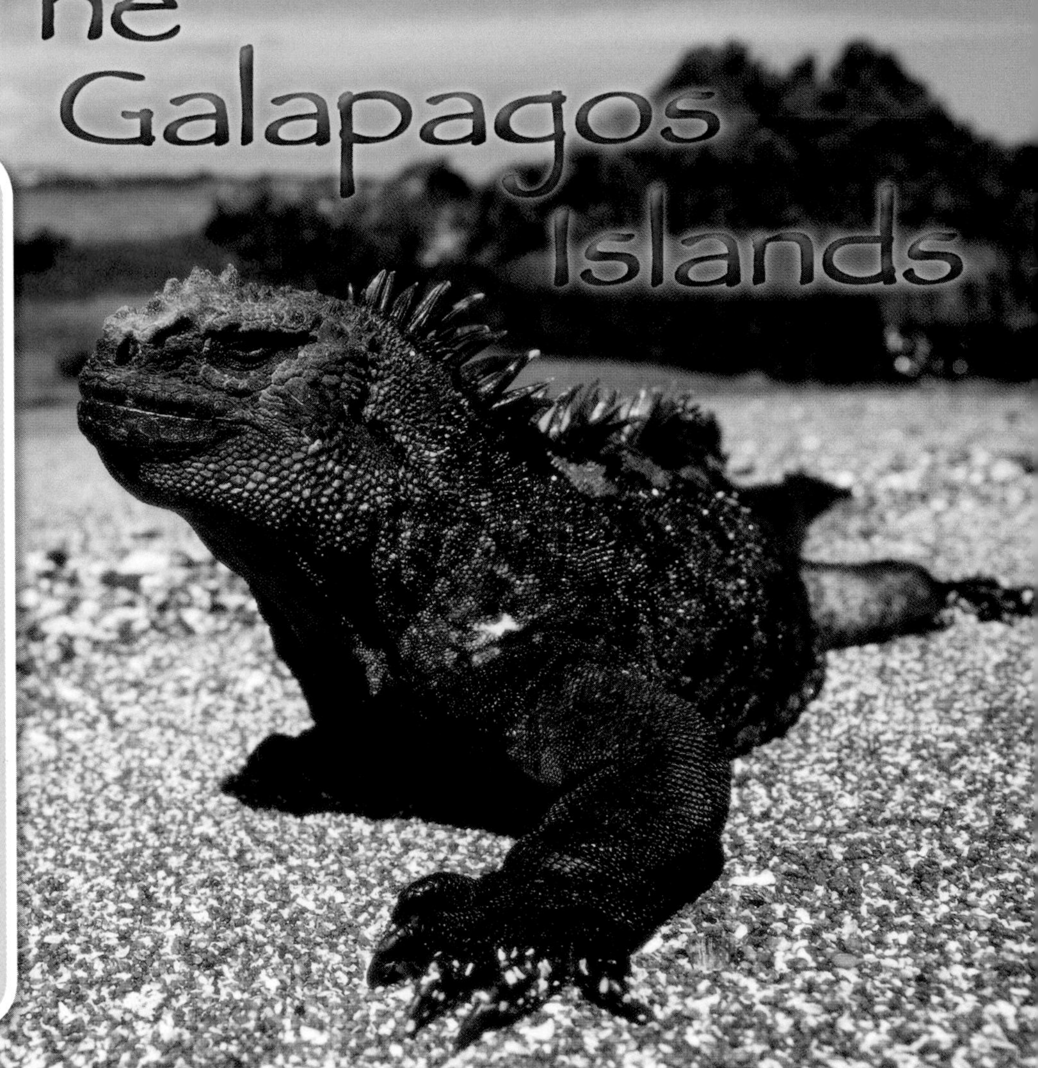

Compare and Contrast in Science

Science writers often **compare** things to show their similarities and **contrast** things to show their differences.

- **Similarity:** *The marine iguana and the giant tortoise are both found only on the Galapagos Islands.*
- **Difference:** *The marine iguana swims into the ocean for food, while the giant tortoise eats plants that grow on land.*

Reader's Guide

distinctive unique

Compare the Galapagos Islands to the Hawaiian Islands.

____

____

____

Use the highlighted sentences and the Reader's Guide to compare and contrast in this article.

Imagine an island where enormous tortoises lie in the sun next to large iguanas. Black-and-white penguins swim alongside brightly colored tropical fish in the ocean. Such a place does exist, but only on the Galapagos Islands. People travel to the islands from all over the world to learn about these **distinctive** plants and animals.

The Galapagos Islands are 600 miles west of the coast of Ecuador in South America. The Galapagos Islands, like the Hawaiian Islands, formed in the Pacific Ocean as a result of volcanic eruptions. Today, the Galapagos include 13 major islands, 6 smaller islands, and dozens of tiny, rocky islands.

Only on the Galapagos Islands

Many of the animals that live on the Galapagos are not found anywhere else in the world. The marine iguana, for example, is the only lizard in the world that swims in the sea. These iguanas live on land, but dive in the ocean to find food. They can stay underwater for as long as 30 minutes before returning to dry land.

The giant tortoise is another animal unique to the Galapagos. These massive creatures eat grass, leaves, and cacti and can weigh 500 pounds or more! Giant tortoises can live to be over 150 years old, older than any other animal on Earth.

Other animals of the Galapagos are more common. However, they have distinctive features that help them live in this colorful and unique place. For example, most penguins live in the cold climate of Antarctica. Scientists were surprised to learn that penguins live in the warm climate of the Galapagos, too. The Galapagos penguin is the only kind of penguin that lives north of the equator. It lives near the cold currents of water that run between some of the islands.

It's not just the animals that fascinate researchers on these **tropical** islands. Of the 560 species of plants on the islands, one third of them can be found only on the Galapagos. The daisy tree, for example, is a sun-loving plant that often forms thick woodlands. Another plant unique to the Galapagos Islands is the lava cactus. This small cactus is different from most plants because it can grow without any soil.

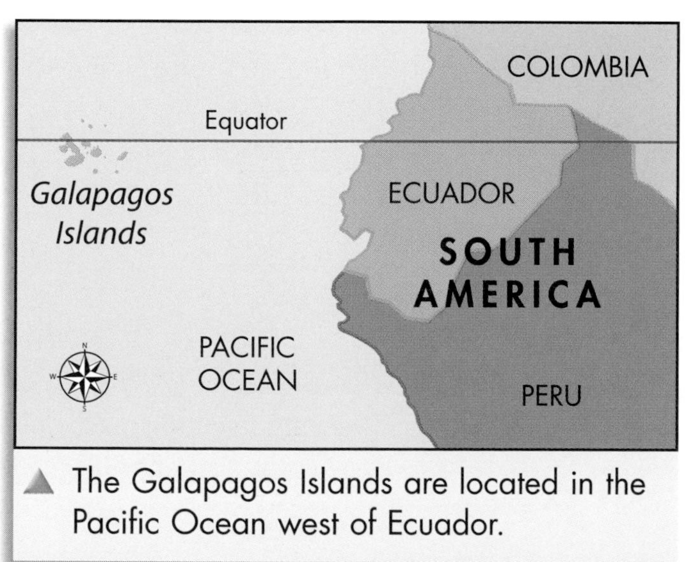

▲ The Galapagos Islands are located in the Pacific Ocean west of Ecuador.

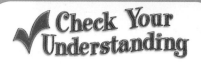

Check Your Understanding

Do you:
- __ picture important details?
- __ look for similarities and differences?

Contrast Galapagos penguins to other penguins in the world.

____

____

____

____

tropical near the equator

How is the lava cactus different from most plants?

____

____

interdependent depending on each other for survival

How do the needs of plants and animals differ?

____

____

____

____

What do native and non-native animals have in common?

____

____

____

Depending on Each Other

Galapagos animals and plants are **interdependent**, that is, they rely on each other to survive. Many animals depend on plants for nourishment. The giant tortoise eats the prickly pear cactus. This plant is very common on the islands, making it a natural choice for food.

Just as the animals depend on the plants to live, the plant life on the islands also depends on the animals for survival. Animals spread plant seeds and pollen over the Galapagos. This ensures that the plants will continue to grow.

Keeping the Galapagos Unique

Although most of the Galapagos Islands are protected as a national park, the plants and animals still face challenges. Over time, people brought new species with them to the islands. These non-native plants and animals caused harm to the native plants and animals, disrupting the islands' unique ecosystem.

Non-native animals, such as goats and donkeys, depend on the same plants as many native animals. By eating the plants on the island, they take food away from the native animals. Other non-native animals, such as pigs and rats, often eat the eggs from the nests of tortoises and sea turtles. This results in fewer births each year. Non-native trees have created large areas of shade where native plants cannot grow.

Scientists are working to protect the native plants and animals of the Galapagos. Researchers and travelers alike are hopeful that their efforts will save the plants and animals of the Galapagos, keeping the islands as unique and colorful as they have always been.

▲ The unique plants and animals of the Galapagos need protection.

Keep Thinking

Think about the article "The Galapagos Islands." Circle the letter next to the best answer.

1. What makes marine iguanas unique?
A They are the only animals that live in the Galapagos.
B They live longer than any other animal on Earth.
C They are the only lizards that swim in the sea.
D They are the only lizards that live in a hot climate.

2. What is the main idea of the article?
A More scientists should study the Galapagos Islands.
B The Galapagos Islands were formed from volcanic eruptions.
C Non-native plants and animals are harmful to the Galapagos Islands.
D The Galapagos Islands are home to many unique plants and animals.

3. The giant tortoise relies on the prickly pear cactus for
A food.
B shelter.
C shade.
D protection.

Write your answers on the lines.

4. How are penguins in the Galapagos different from those in Antarctica?

____

____

5. What threat do native animals and plants face on the Galapagos Islands?

____

____

6. **Contrast** the Galapagos Islands today with the way they were before people introduced other plants and animals.

____

____

____

Get Organized

Fill in the graphic organizer to compare and contrast plant life and animal life on the Galapagos Islands.

Plant Life	Animal Life
1. One third of the plants there exist only on the Galapagos.	1. ______
2. ______	2. Animals depend on plants for food.

Plant and Animal Life
1. Both include many species that are unique to the Galapagos Islands.
2. ______
3. ______

Summarize

Imagine that you have visited the Galapagos Islands to study the unique plant and animal life. Write the first paragraph of a newspaper article about your trip.

______

______

______

______

Write Away!

Team Up

Suppose that you and your partner are planning a research trip to the Galapagos Islands. List two plants or animals that you want to study, and explain your reasons.

1. ____

____

2. ____

____

On Your Own

Imagine that you have just returned from a research trip to the Galapagos Islands. Write a speech about your trip. **Compare** and **contrast** the plants and animals you studied. Try to persuade your audience to help preserve the islands.

WRITER'S CHECKLIST

- ☐ Describe your trip and the unique features of the Galapagos Islands.
- ☐ Compare and contrast the plants and animals you studied.
- ☐ Be persuasive. Convince listeners to help preserve the Galapagos.

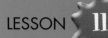

LESSON 11

Different Islands, Different Lives

Compare and Contrast in Social Studies

Social studies articles often **compare** and **contrast** to show the ways people, things, or places are similar or different. One way writers do this is by showing advantages and disadvantages.

- **Disadvantage:** *Bermuda has very little drinking water.*
- **Advantage:** *Roofs on the island are designed to catch rainwater and save it for drinking.*

Reader's Guide

natural resources useful materials occurring in nature

What are two disadvantages that most islands have?

1. ______________________

____

2. ______________________

____

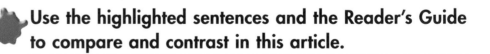

Use the highlighted sentences and the Reader's Guide to compare and contrast in this article.

Not all islands are tropical paradises, and life isn't easy even on islands that *are*. Most islands have delicate environments and few **natural resources**. Bermuda, Iceland, and Madagascar are islands with much in common, but they have some important differences, too. How do the people on these islands create a workable way of life?

Bermuda

Bermuda is a tropical island in the Atlantic Ocean. Its total area is a little more than 20 square miles, about the size of Manhattan in New York City. The island is home to about 65,500 Bermudians.

Bermuda is made up of one large main island and more than one hundred very small coral islands. The land is fairly flat, with low hills and green valleys. The island gets some rainfall, but unlike Iceland or Madagascar, it has no freshwater rivers or lakes. Rainwater doesn't collect on land. It seeps into the limestone that makes up the islands.

To make up for this disadvantage, houses on Bermuda are designed to collect rainwater. The roofs are made of limestone shingles that channel rainwater into underground water tanks. There is no central water system on the island, so each home has its own tank. Because of air pollution, a law requires homeowners to regularly paint their roofs with special paint called whitewash. This ensures that pollution won't build up on the roofs and pollute the water.

What is a disadvantage of living in Bermuda?

____

____

Check Your Understanding

Do you:
- __ find advantages and disadvantages?
- __ look for main ideas and details?

Iceland

Iceland is located in the Atlantic Ocean just south of the Arctic Circle. About 300,000 Icelanders live on its 39,000 square miles, slightly smaller than the state of Kentucky.

Iceland is covered in many places by glaciers. The climate along the coast is **temperate**, but almost none of the land in Iceland can be farmed. Land that isn't under ice is likely to be very hot—active volcanoes are located all over the island. Rain seeps into the volcanic rock, and the underground lava heats the water. This process creates hot pools of water, which look like steaming lakes.

temperate a climate that doesn't get very hot or cold

Use the highlighted sentences on this page to **contrast** the land in Bermuda with the land in Iceland.

Bermuda ______________________________

____

____

Iceland ______________________________

____

____

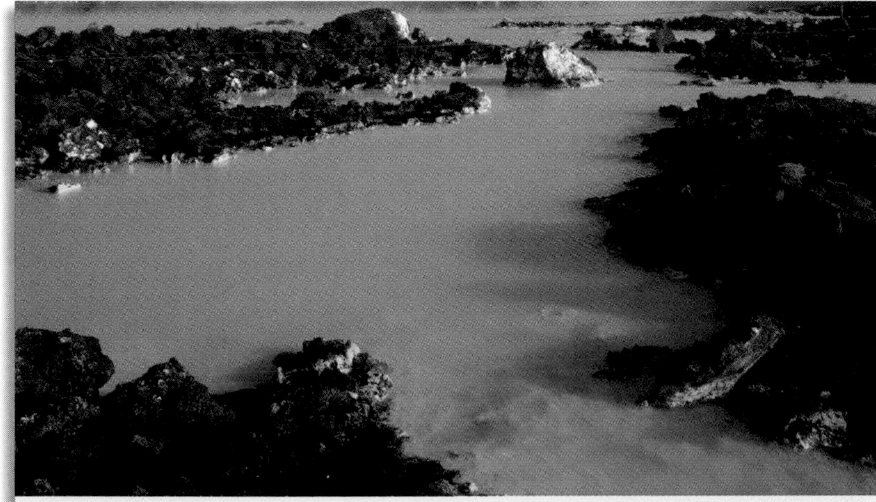

▲ In Iceland, water heated by underground lava forms steaming pools.

geothermal energy heat that comes from inside Earth

Homes make the most of the **geothermal energy** in Iceland. Almost 90 percent of the houses in Iceland are heated by volcanic hot water. Houses don't need furnaces that burn gas or oil for heat. They have radiators that fill with the hot water from underground and keep the houses warm.

Madagascar

Madagascar is the fourth-largest island in the world. At just over 226,000 square miles, it's almost twice as big as Arizona. Madagascar is located in the Indian Ocean, 250 miles east of mainland Africa. There are more than 18 million people, known as Malagasy, living on the island.

Madagascar has both plains and mountains. The climate is warm and humid near the sea, temperate inland, and hot and dry in the south.

Contrast Madagascar's different climates.

____

____

____

____

Houses in the countryside are usually made of palm leaves or sticks plastered with mud, and the roofs are thatched. Most houses are on stilts so that rice harvests can be stored underneath. City dwellers often have homes made of baked bricks.

Madagascar has thousands of miles of roads, but most of them are unpaved and in poor condition. As a result, many people travel by canoe. Malagasy can use the boats to fish, do their errands, and visit friends.

What is an advantage and disadvantage of travel in Madagascar?

Advantage: ____________________

____

____

Disadvantage: _________________

____

____

▲ Many Malagasy travel in a special type of canoe.

Every island has its advantages and disadvantages. Drinking water may be scarce, but roofs can be water-catchers. Roads may be hard to travel, but canoes can provide transportation. When people find solutions to limited resources, island life really can be paradise.

Keep Thinking

Think about the article "Different Islands, Different Lives." Circle the letter next to the best answer.

1. What do Iceland and Bermuda have in common?
- **A** Both islands use geothermal energy.
- **B** Both islands have no freshwater rivers or lakes.
- **C** Both islands are covered in many places by glaciers.
- **D** Both islands are located in the Atlantic Ocean.

2. Based on the article, make an inference about people who choose to live on islands.
- **A** They are forced to build special houses.
- **B** They don't need to work to earn a living.
- **C** They make the most of the island's resources.
- **D** They must own boats instead of cars.

3. What caused Bermuda's government to pass a law about painting roofs regularly?
- **A** The roofs have to be able to catch rainwater.
- **B** Unclean roofs could pollute the water.
- **C** Whitewash keeps the shingles from cracking.
- **D** Fresh paint helps to reflect the hot sun.

Write your answers on the lines.

4. Write a sentence that **compares** Iceland and Madagascar.

____

____

____

5. Write a sentence that **contrasts** Bermuda and Madagascar.

____

____

____

6. Which island, in your opinion, would be most difficult for you to live on? Why?

____

____

____

Get Organized

Fill in the charts with one advantage and one disadvantage for each of the three islands.

Bermuda

Advantage: The roofs are designed to catch rainwater.

Disadvantage: ______

Iceland

Advantage: ______

Disadvantage: ______

Madagascar

Advantage: ______

Disadvantage: ______

Summarize

Imagine that you are one of the original settlers of Bermuda in 1609. Write a journal entry describing the challenges that you will face as you set out to make Bermuda your home.

______

Write Away!

Team Up

Work with a partner. Imagine that your class has the chance to travel to either Bermuda, Iceland, or Madagascar. Which island would you choose? **Compare** and **contrast** the islands, and explain your choice.

On Your Own

Imagine that your class really went to the island you chose above. Write a letter home describing the island. **Compare** and **contrast** life at home with life on the island.

WRITER'S CHECKLIST

- ☐ Write a friendly letter.
- ☐ Use details to describe the island.
- ☐ Include information about the island's advantages and disadvantages.
- ☐ Tell the ways life on the island is similar to or different from life at home.

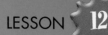

LESSON 12

Island Tides

Compare and Contrast in Math

In math, readers can **compare** and **contrast** the information that numbers give them. For example, the time and height of low tides can help island dwellers plan when to run on the beach or collect seashells.

A line graph can help people compare and contrast the time and height of the low tide each day.

Gather Information **An island's shoreline usually gets two high tides and two low tides each day. The times and heights of the tides change from day to day. Study the tide chart below to learn the time and height of the first low tide on Marco Island each day for one week.**

First Low Tide

Day	Tide Time	Height in Feet
Sunday	7:15 A.M.	0.4
Monday	8:01 A.M.	0.2
Tuesday	8:47 A.M.	0.0
Wednesday	9:34 A.M.	0.0
Thursday	10:25 A.M.	0.2
Friday	11:23 A.M.	0.4
Saturday	12:33 P.M.	0.6

Understand a Line Graph **A line graph helps readers compare and contrast the time at which low tides occur each day. Use the line graph below and the tide chart to answer the questions.**

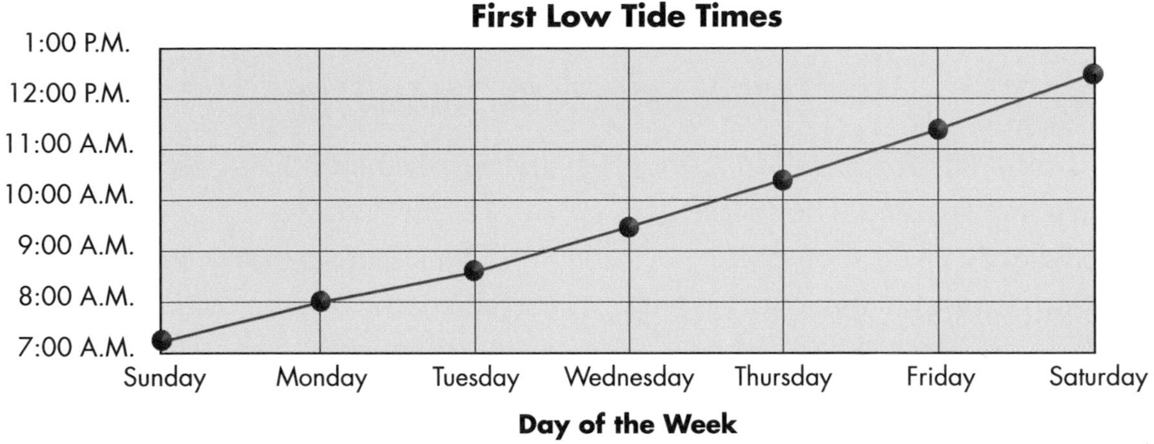

1. What pattern do you see in the low tides by studying the line graph?

____

2. **Contrast** Saturday's low tide with Friday's. How much later is Saturday's tide?

____

3. At what time do you think the following Sunday's tide would happen? Why?

____

____

Make Your Own Line Graph **Use the tide chart to complete the line graph below with the height of the first low tide each day.**

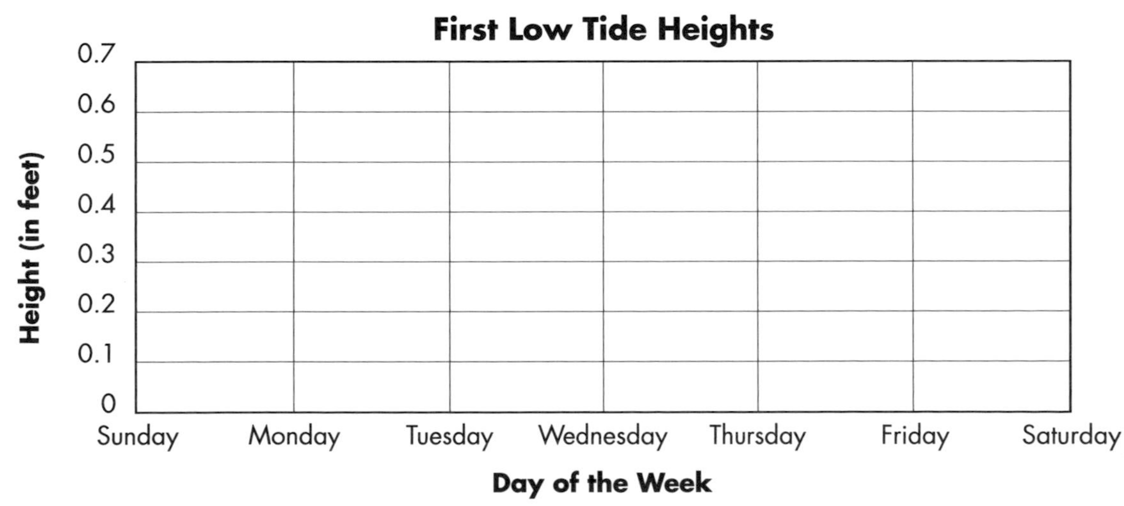

Making Connections

Read the article below. Then answer the questions.

The Mysterious Island

One of the most famous islands in history may have never even existed. The ancient Greeks wrote about a civilization called Atlantis, but no one knows if the story is true.

According to the Greek legend, Atlantis was an island located in the middle of the world's oceans. It had gardens and temples covered in silver and gold, and crowded in its harbors were merchant ships from all over the world.

The ancient legend told that Zeus, the most powerful of all the Greek gods, thought the people of Atlantis were getting greedy. As a result, he decided to punish them. According to the Greek legend, around 9600 B.C., the ground rumbled and the island of Atlantis sank into the sea.

If Atlantis was a real place, then what happened to it? Some scientists think that a meteorite could have fallen from the sky and smashed into the island, destroying it completely.

Other scientists think that a strong earthquake or volcano could have caused a giant ocean wave, or tsunami. The tsunami may have flooded Atlantis, leaving only ruins under the ocean.

No one is sure what happened to Atlantis. People continue to search for the lost civilization by exploring underwater ruins and learning what they can from the past. What do you think about this mysterious island? Was it real or just make-believe?

1. According to legend, what was Atlantis like before and after 9600 B.C.?

____

____

2. **Contrast** two of the ways Atlantis could have been destroyed.

____

____

3. How was Atlantis the same as all other islands?

____

Apply Your Knowledge **Think about the story "Island Castaways" and the articles you have read in this unit. Answer the questions below.**

Imagine that you are stranded on a deserted island. In what ways would island life be different from your life today?

____

____

What three things would you bring with you to make island living easier? Explain why you would choose to bring each one.

Item 1: ______________

Item 2: ______________

Item 3: ______________

Choose a Team Project **Choose one of the following group activities, and complete it using your knowledge of islands.**

Map Your Own Island

Suppose that your group is stranded on an unknown island. Draw a map of the island and label at least five of its major resources. Then discuss the different ways you will use each of the resources to survive on the island. Include the explanations on your map. Give your island a name, and add it as the map's title. Share your island map with the class.

Create a Web Site

With your group, choose one of the islands from this unit, and plan a new Web site that tells people about this island. Work together to create the home page, and then have each member of your group write a different section of the site. Include the ways your island is similar to or different from other islands. Present your Web site to the class.

Summarize in Fiction

A **summary** is a short description of the most important events in a story. To summarize a story, think about the story elements, which include characters, plot, and setting.

The story elements can help readers answer questions about a story, such as *who, what, where, when, why,* and *how*.

Flying to Victory

Reader's Guide

Use the chart to **summarize** the most important information from the highlighted paragraph.

Who?	Tony
What?	________ ________
Where?	________
When?	________

Use the highlighted sentences and the Reader's Guide to summarize this story.

"You have a message from Rita," said the computer.

Tony slid out from underneath his small racing jet, *Wind-Walker*, and put down his tools. "Open message," he said to the computer, and the large computer screen on the wall filled with tiny bits of 3-D confetti. Huge words bounced across the screen, saying, "YOU MADE THE CUT!" Tony leaned against the *Wind-Walker*, smiling. He had done it!

It was the year 3007, and time for the annual Junior Flight Competition. Young people from all over the world built their small jets, or skiffs, to compete in the fastest airborne race on Earth. The weekend before, Tony had piloted his skiff on a test course near his home in New Chicago. Judges had recorded his time and compared it to the times of other pilots around the world. Now he had made the cut and was going to the big race in Hawaii.

A week later, Tony, his best friend Rita, and all four parents boarded the crowded transport shuttle to Hawaii. After three hours, the shuttle landed at the air terminal in Hawaii, which was full of shuttles from all over the world. Tony's group immediately went to the track to register for the competition. Mechanics were busy wheeling in all of the skiffs, placing each in a separate stall.

Tony felt sure that most of the skiffs in the competition had been built by professionals. One had a hydro-drive, which converted the moisture in clouds into a boost of power, and another skiff had a radio guidance system, which enabled a computer to fly the jet almost entirely by itself. Some of the skiffs were even sponsored by big companies.

Tony had spent months constructing the *Wind-Walker* in his garage with his friend, Rita. Rita was an engineering whiz and knew almost everything about airspeed, altitude, and jet engines.

The night before the big race, Tony and Rita decided that the *Wind-Walker* needed a little extra work to help it keep up with the impressive competition. That night, they worked in their stall, tinkering with the skiff.

It grew late, and Tony's hands got so tired that they trembled as he worked. As he pried the covering off the scramjet, a turbo engine that worked only at the highest speeds, his fingers slipped, and the cover slammed down on his hand.

"My hand!" Tony yelled. The pain was intense as he tried to move his fingers, but he quickly blinked back his tears.

Summarize what the highlighted paragraph suggests about the setting.

____

____

____

Check Your Understanding

Do you:

__ read to find story elements?

__ summarize as you read?

Summarize the highlighted paragraph in one sentence.

____

____

____

Summarize the highlighted paragraph by filling in the story elements.

Characters: ______________

____

Setting: ______________

____

Plot: ______________

____

____

Write one sentence that **summarizes** what made Rita a good pilot.

____

____

____

____

"Rita, if I can't use my hand, I can't fly the skiff tomorrow. I need my hand to work the control bar," Tony said. Then he said to his friend desperately, "There's only one thing to do—you're going to have to fly the *Wind-Walker*."

Rita looked shocked. "Me? I can't fly it. I've never even flown before!"

"You know as much as I do," Tony said. "You designed it! You probably know how to fly it better than I do."

Rita looked at the skiff and then at Tony's hand. She thought for a minute and realized that he was right. "All right. Let's get to work," she said.

The next morning, the stands were packed with fans. The racecourse was marked by floating pods that blinked with red lights. The skiffs roared up to the starting line—the race was about to begin.

Rita sat behind the control bar of the *Wind-Walker* and gave Tony the thumbs-up. She had practiced for hours and felt as ready as she'd ever be. Tony stood in the stands with his injured hand wrapped in a thick bandage. The starting signal buzzed, and with a roar, all of the skiffs took off. They soared toward the blue of the ocean and then straightened out, screaming over the waves.

Rita kept her hands firmly on the control bar. She knew everything about the way the *Wind-Walker* worked, and probably almost everything about the way the other skiffs worked, too. With every turn she kept one second ahead, and with every dive she picked up speed.

Then, in the final lap, as the *Wind-Walker* swooped down over a rocky cliff, Rita pressed the scramjet button. The skiff burst forward with a loud scream, carrying the new Junior Flight Champion right over the finish line.

Keep Thinking

Think about the story "Flying to Victory." Circle the letter next to the best answer.

1. Which new title best **summarizes** this story?
   A Life in New Chicago
   B Tony: A Master Mechanic
   C Teamwork Wins the Race
   D Taking the Shuttle to Hawaii

2. Which sentence best contrasts Tony and Rita?
   A Tony lived in New Chicago, but Rita lived in Hawaii.
   B Tony was a good pilot, but Rita was an engineering whiz.
   C Tony did not make the cut, but Rita did.
   D Tony and Rita were both great engineers.

3. What happened right *before* Rita agreed to pilot the *Wind-Walker*?
   A Rita learned to fly the skiff.
   B Rita and Tony won the test race.
   C Tony hurt his hand.
   D Tony and Rita arrived in Hawaii.

Write your answers on the lines.

4. Write a sentence that describes the setting of the racecourse.

___

___

5. Who were the main characters in the story? **Summarize** the most important information about each one.

___

___

6. **Summarize** what happened at the beginning, middle, and end of the story.

___

___

___

Get Organized

Fill in the graphic organizer with descriptions of the story elements in "Flying to Victory."

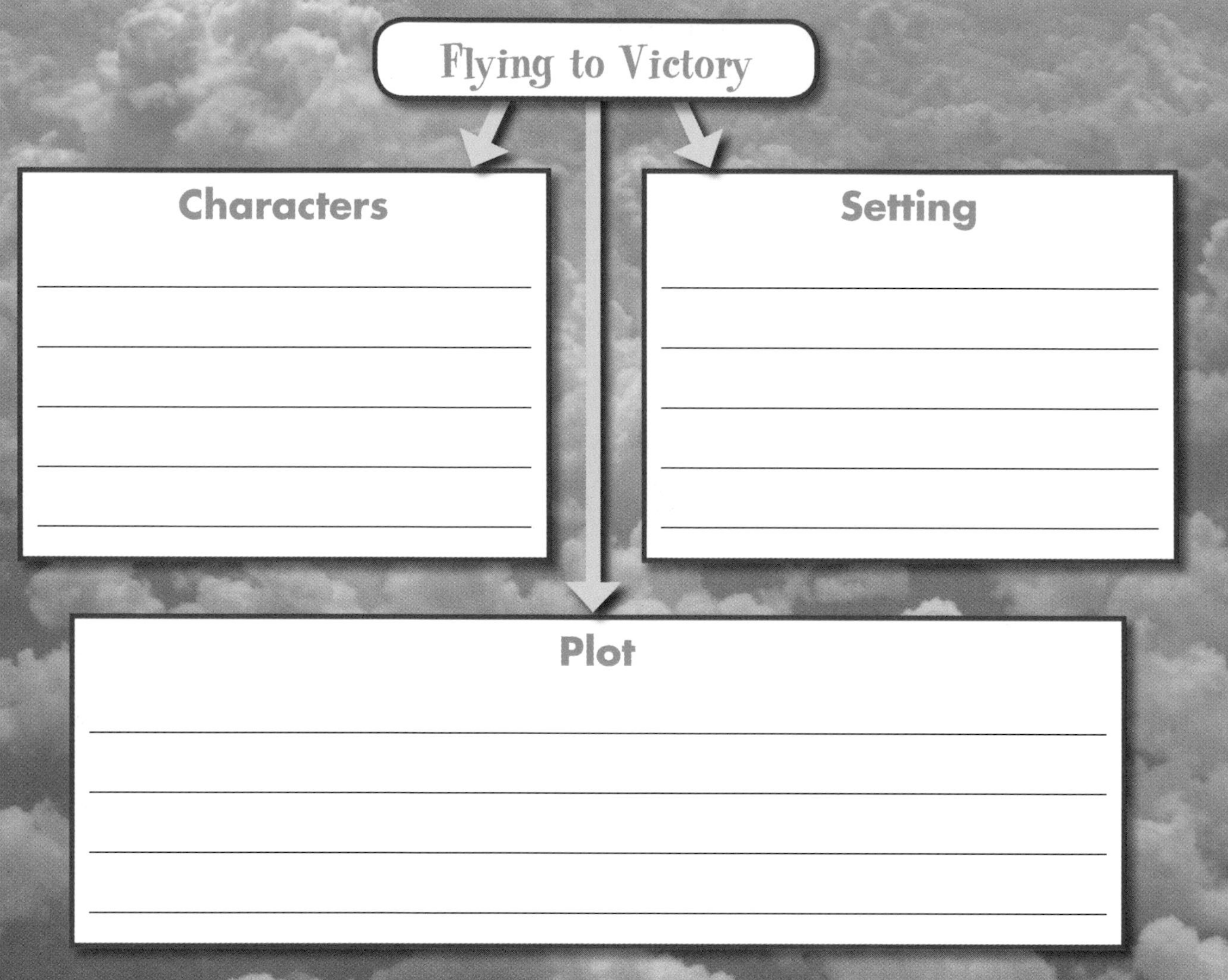

Summarize

Imagine that you are a journalist for *Turbo Times,* a skiff-racing magazine. Write a **summary** of what happened during the Junior Flight Competition.

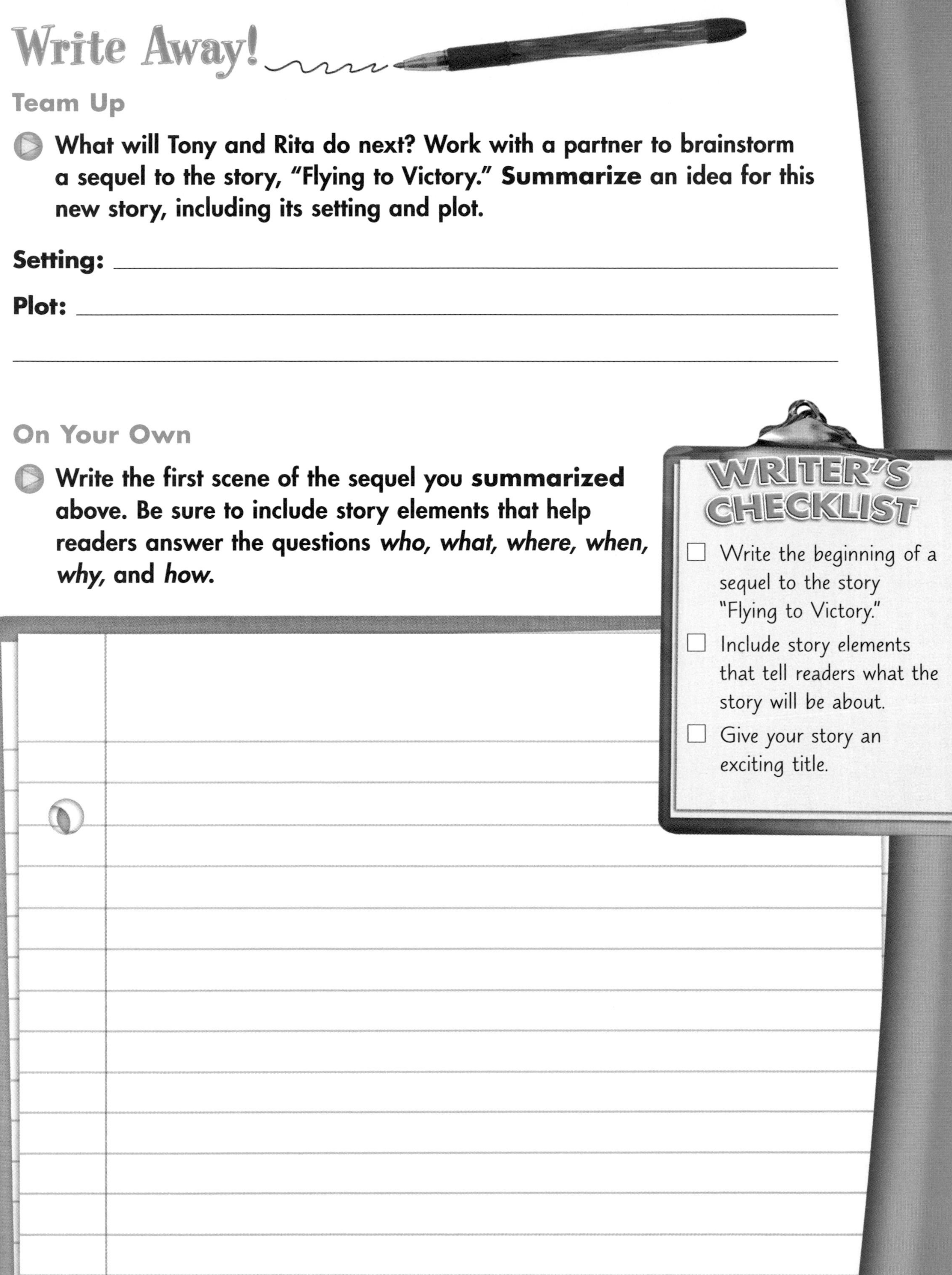

Write Away!

Team Up

What will Tony and Rita do next? Work with a partner to brainstorm a sequel to the story, "Flying to Victory." **Summarize** an idea for this new story, including its setting and plot.

Setting: ______________________________

Plot: ______________________________

____

On Your Own

Write the first scene of the sequel you **summarized** above. Be sure to include story elements that help readers answer the questions *who, what, where, when, why,* and *how.*

WRITER'S CHECKLIST
☐ Write the beginning of a sequel to the story "Flying to Victory."
☐ Include story elements that tell readers what the story will be about.
☐ Give your story an exciting title.

LESSON 14

Airplane Technology Takes Off

Summarize in Science

Science articles are full of interesting facts. The most important information can be used to **summarize** the main points of the article.

Headings give clues about the most important information in each section. Summarizing as you read can help you understand and remember the most important information.

Reader's Guide

What does the highlighted **summary** sentence suggest the article will be about?

___

___

atmosphere the gases surrounding a planet

Use the highlighted sentences and the Reader's Guide to summarize this article.

The crowd of excited onlookers waited in the desert heat to catch a glimpse of the landing. They cheered loudly as the plane safely touched down. Minutes earlier, SpaceShipOne had soared at a record-breaking height of 62 miles above Earth. It was the highest that any airplane had ever flown. SpaceShipOne is just one of many recent advances in flight technology that are changing the way we fly.

Blasting into Space

Before SpaceShipOne made its first flight into space, only government astronauts had blasted through Earth's **atmosphere**. But in June 2004, SpaceShipOne made history. It became the first airplane to fly into space.

The new aircraft makes it easier to reach space. Its creators hope it will make more space travel possible in the future.

The task wasn't easy, however. It took more than three years and seven failed test flights before the engineering team finally succeeded. One challenge they faced was that the fuel needed to blast through the atmosphere weighed the plane down. The team designed the White Knight aircraft to solve this problem. This airplane could carry SpaceShipOne to 50,000 feet, allowing SpaceShipOne to carry less fuel.

Another problem was that **friction** with the air molecules in Earth's atmosphere threatened to burn up the craft. To prevent this problem, engineers designed the wings of the craft to fold in a way that slows it down. When SpaceShipOne is safely inside Earth's atmosphere, the wings unfold to help the craft glide safely to the ground.

friction rubbing that causes heat

Summarize the most important information in the highlighted paragraph.

____

____

____

Jumbo Jet

While some engineers had their eyes on space, others focused on the latest technology in passenger aircraft. In January 2005, the airplane company Airbus built the first A380, the largest passenger plane ever made. The aircraft weighs 464 tons. It can carry a total of 840 passengers on two different levels. From head to tail, it measures the length of a football field. To land, it uses twenty wheels.

Write a new heading that **summarizes** this paragraph.

____

____

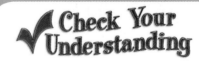

▲ The Airbus A380 is the largest commercial airplane ever built.

Check Your Understanding

Do you:

__ read section headings?

__ summarize the main ideas of each section as you read?

aerodynamic shaped to move easily through air

Use the heading to predict the most important information in this section.

____

____

____

Write one sentence to **summarize** the highlighted paragraph.

____

____

____

Size isn't the only impressive feature of the Airbus A380, however. The engineers of the plane also claim that the jets are quieter and more efficient than those on smaller planes. Its lighter materials and **aerodynamic** design make this jumbo jet a technological wonder.

Remote Controlled

In contrast with the Airbus A380, the latest technology in flight is an airplane that carries no one, not even a pilot. Unmanned Aerial Vehicles, or UAVs, are now being built and tested. UAVs work like any other small airplane, only they have an antenna that allows the plane to be controlled from the ground.

Planes that don't contain people can fly into areas that are considered extremely dangerous. The Predator, for example, is a type of unmanned spy plane that was built to fly over enemy territory. The Altair is a similar UAV built for scientific research. Engineers hope that UAVs will be able to do things other planes can't, such as collecting information from the center of a volcano or tornado.

▲ Look carefully. What's missing from the Altair?

Flight technology has come a long way since the first airplane flown by the Wright brothers in 1903. Since then, engineers and pilots have kept testing the limits of flight. As a result, flight technology continues to reach new heights.

Keep Thinking

Think about the story "Airplane Technology Takes Off." Circle the letter next to the best answer.

1. Which sentence best **summarizes** the article?
- **A** UAVs can fly in conditions that are too dangerous for pilots.
- **B** SpaceShipOne is changing the future of space flight.
- **C** Airplane technology is becoming more advanced.
- **D** Engineers have found ways for planes to take off without runways.

2. Why did engineers build an airplane that flies into space?
- **A** They want more people to be able to travel into space.
- **B** The space shuttle doesn't fly high enough.
- **C** They want to help astronauts reach Mars.
- **D** Earth's atmosphere was threatening to burn up.

3. How is the Airbus A380 different from other airplanes?
- **A** The A380 needs wheels to land.
- **B** The A380 takes up less room.
- **C** The A380 does not have a pilot.
- **D** The A380 is bigger and quieter.

Write your answers on the lines.

4. Write a sentence that **summarizes** one way that airplane technology has changed.

____

____

5. In one sentence, **summarize** the advantages of unmanned airplanes.

____

____

6. Write a **summary** of the section "Blasting into Space."

____

____

____

____

Get Organized

Fill in the graphic organizer to **summarize** the two most important ideas in each section of the article.

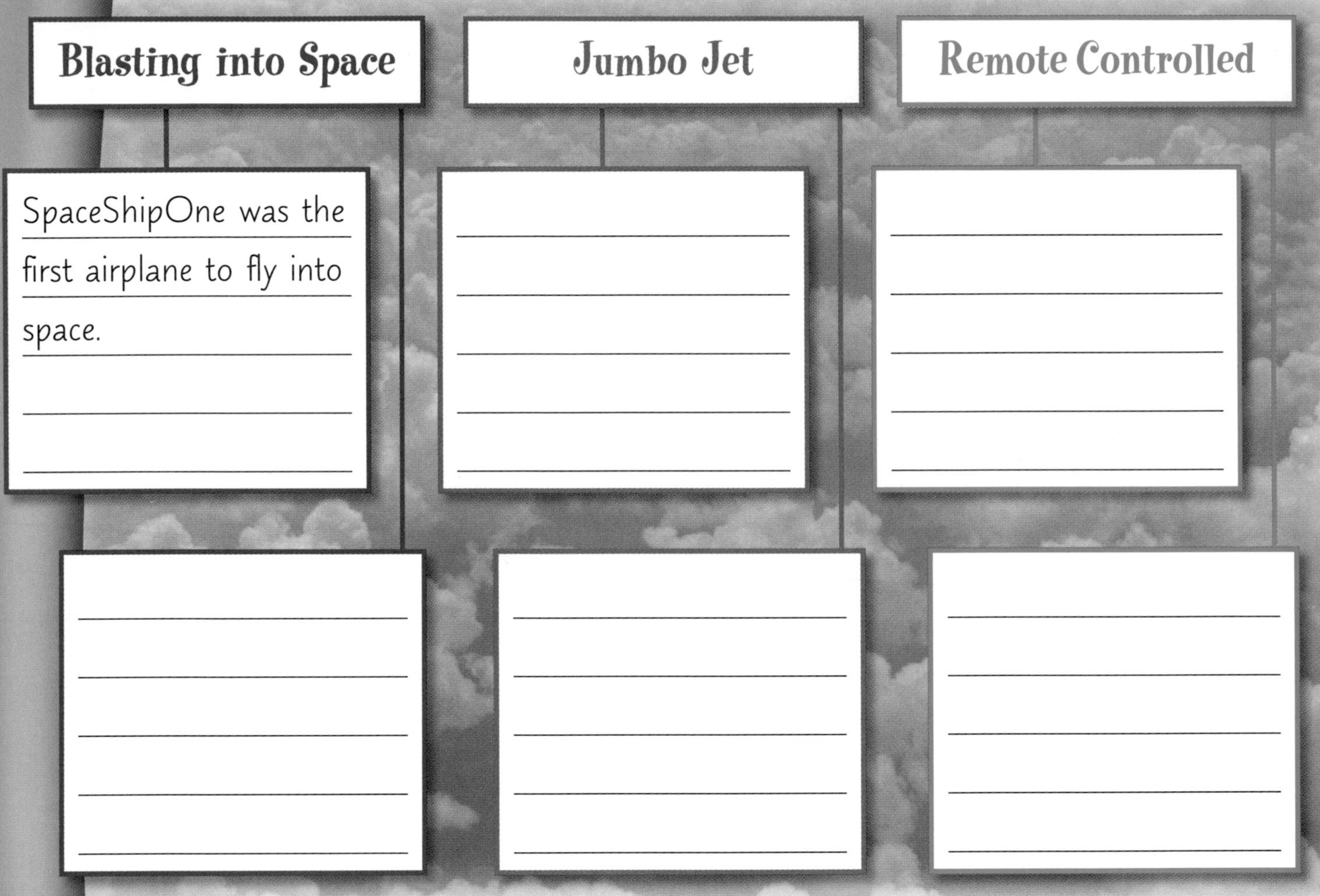

Blasting into Space
Jumbo Jet
Remote Controlled
SpaceShipOne was the first airplane to fly into space.

Summarize

Imagine that you are entering a contest to win a ride on SpaceShipOne. To enter, you must briefly describe modern flight technology. Write the **summary** below.

Write Away!

Team Up

Work with a partner. Discuss which advance in flight technology you think is most important. **Summarize** your reasons below.

On Your Own

Imagine that you were a spectator at the first successful SpaceShipOne flight. Your best friend missed the historic event. Write a letter to your friend, **summarizing** the flight from takeoff to landing.

WRITER'S CHECKLIST

- ☐ Write a friendly letter.
- ☐ Imagine what it would have been like to witness the event.
- ☐ Use important details from the article to summarize the flight from takeoff to landing.

LESSON 15

Up, Up, and Away!

Summarize in Social Studies

Social studies articles often describe important events. To **summarize** an article, readers must distinguish the essential information from the less important information.

While reading an article, readers can find and underline the essential information by answering the questions *who, what, where, when, why,* and *how*. Then the underlined information can be used to summarize the article.

Reader's Guide

adventurer someone who takes part in exciting or risky activities

Underline the essential information that describes *who, what, where,* and *when*.

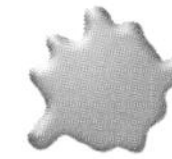

Use the highlighted sentences and the Reader's Guide to summarize this article.

On a crisp winter's day, January 9, 1793, a crowd gathered in Philadelphia, Pennsylvania. French **adventurer** Jean-Pierre Blanchard was about to make history by becoming the first person to fly in the United States. He wasn't in an airplane. This first American flight took place in a balloon.

Launching into History

For years, people had dreamed about flying in the sky. Ten years before Blanchard's American adventure, a group of passengers in France had already tested a balloon flight. However, the passengers weren't people—they were a duck, a sheep, and a rooster! The balloon was made of paper and fabric and filled with hot air. The flight only lasted eight minutes before the three passengers safely returned to the ground almost two miles away.

The engineers of this 1783 balloon flight were brothers, Joseph and Jacques Montgolfier. Within two months, the first human passengers had flown in a Montgolfier balloon. They traveled more than five miles in a trip that lasted 25 minutes.

Write one sentence to **summarize** the highlighted paragraph.

___

___

___

The Montgolfier brothers inspired others to pursue ballooning. One of the most successful of these inventors was Jean-Pierre Blanchard. People did not trust the safety of balloons, so Blanchard demonstrated the use of the first parachute. As with the test balloon flight, an animal was the first to safely take a parachute ride. Later, Blanchard himself successfully parachuted from a balloon.

▲ The first human balloon flight took place in France in 1783.

Check Your Understanding

Do you:

_ underline important information as you read?

_ distinguish between essential and less important information?

The United States Lifts Off

The most memorable of Blanchard's **accomplishments** was that first U.S. balloon flight in 1793. Instead of flying a balloon filled with hot air like the Montgolfier brothers, Blanchard's balloon was filled with hydrogen, a gas much lighter than air.

accomplishments remarkable or successful achievements

Underline the most important information in the highlighted paragraph.

Blanchard planned to take off from Philadelphia at exactly 10:00 on the morning of January 9, 1793. At 9:45, a carriage drove up carrying the President of the United States, George Washington. The President presented Blanchard with a letter to act as a legal passport for his air travel. The letter is now considered the first piece of U.S. airmail.

What is the most essential information in this paragraph?

Underline the essential information in the highlighted paragraph, and write a brief **summary** below.

A woman in the crowd handed Blanchard a small dog to accompany him on the trip. As Blanchard's balloon began to rise, one of Washington's generals remarked that it "was the most interesting sight that I ever beheld."

Blanchard's balloon met a mild northwest breeze as it leveled off at an altitude of about 5,800 feet. During his flight, Blanchard recorded several scientific measurements in his log. As he drifted through the air, he even had a small snack.

When Blanchard saw the Atlantic Ocean in the distance, he began his descent, slowly releasing hydrogen from the balloon. The flight took about 45 minutes and ended in New Jersey, 15 miles from where Blanchard had started. The first U.S. balloon flight was a complete success.

In New Jersey, Blanchard was met by a crowd of confused farmers who had never seen such a strange flying machine. Blanchard won them over by offering the puzzled onlookers food and the President's letter. This pleased the farmers, and they helped him get back to Philadelphia.

▲ The first U.S. balloon flight was in 1793.

Flying into the Future

That evening, Blanchard returned to Philadelphia to a mob of admirers. The flight had a strong effect on all of its viewers. It demonstrated to many people the importance of human flight.

Blanchard could not have known the great strides in **aeronautics** that would take place in the United States over the next two hundred years, but he surely inspired many future Americans to take to the sky.

aeronautics the science of building and operating aircraft

Keep Thinking

Think about the article "Up, Up, and Away!" Circle the letter next to the best answer.

1. Which is the best **summary** of the article?
   A Blanchard's balloon flight lasted about 45 minutes.
   B The first balloon flights were important steps in the history of flight.
   C The Montgolfier brothers engineered the first balloon ride.
   D Much has changed in aeronautics over the past two hundred years.

2. How were Blanchard's and the Montgolfier brothers' balloons different?
   A They were filled with different gases.
   B Blanchard's was safe, but the Montgolfiers' was not.
   C Blanchard's was made for animals, but the Montgolfiers' was made for people.
   D They were no differences between the two balloons.

3. Which detail shows that Blanchard's flight was an important event?
   A Blanchard had a dog with him.
   B Blanchard's flight lasted about 45 minutes.
   C President George Washington attended.
   D Farmers in New Jersey helped Blanchard.

Write your answers on the lines.

4. Write a new heading that **summarizes** the section "The United States Lifts Off."

____

____

5. **Summarize** the first balloon flight of the Montgolfier brothers.

____

____

____

6. Write one detail from the article that would NOT be essential to include in a **summary**.

____

____

Get Organized

Complete the chart to **summarize** the first U.S. balloon flight.

Who?	French adventurer Jean-Pierre Blanchard
What?	
Where?	
When?	
Why?	
How?	

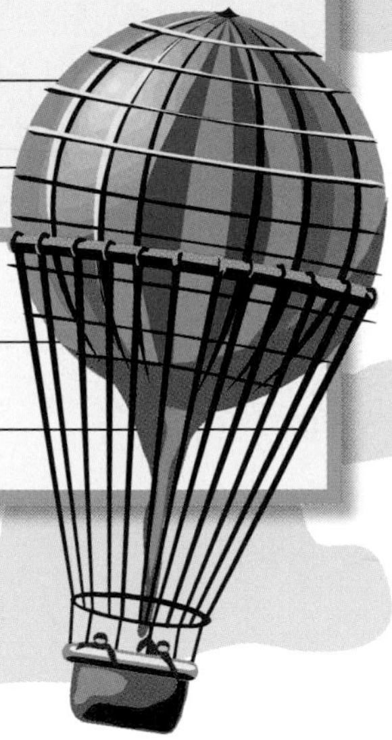

Summarize

Imagine that you are a reporter covering Blanchard's 1793 flight. Write a **summary** that you would report in the local newspaper. Use the chart above to help you.

Write Away!

Team Up

Imagine that you and a partner are planning a trip around the world in a balloon. **Summarize** the essential information about your trip below.

On Your Own

Write a press release that **summarizes** your plans for an around-the-world balloon trip. Answer the questions *who, what, where, when, why,* and *how.*

WRITER'S CHECKLIST

- ☐ Write a press release that reporters will use to write news articles.
- ☐ Summarize your plans for an around-the-world balloon trip.
- ☐ Include information that answers the questions *who, what, where, when, why,* and *how.*

Summarize in Math

In math, numbers can **summarize** the most important information. A pilot's log, for example, summarizes important information about a flight. The flight log is a place where a pilot can record what happened during a flight.

Flight Logs

Gather Information **The Wright brothers were the first people to build and fly a motor-powered airplane. Wilbur and Orville Wright also kept one of the earliest flight logs. The flight log below summarizes their first successful flights at Kitty Hawk, North Carolina, in 1903.**

The Wright Brothers' First Flights

Flight	Pilot	Time	Distance	Altitude
1	Orville Wright	12 seconds	120 feet	8–10 feet
2	Wilbur Wright	12 seconds	175 feet	unknown
3	Orville Wright	15 seconds	200 feet	12–14 feet
4	Wilbur Wright	59 seconds	852 feet	unknown

Understand a Bar Graph

A bar graph can present a summary of the distance flown by the Wright Brothers' airplane. Study the bar graph. Then use the bar graph and the flight log to answer the questions.

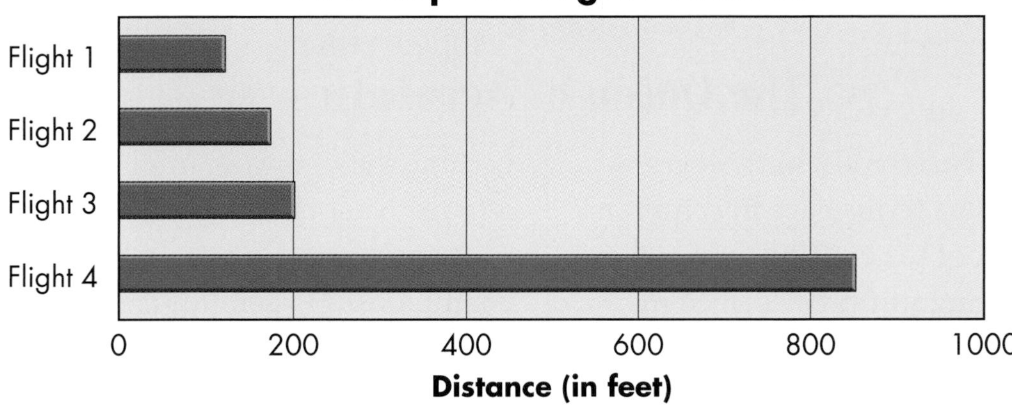

1. Using the bar graph, about how many feet longer was flight 4 than flight 3?

____

2. Add the distances in the flight log to find the total distance of all four flights.

____

3. **Summarize** the most important information from the bar graph and flight log.

____

____

Make Your Own Bar Graph

Complete the bar graph to show how long each of the first four flights lasted. Then write a sentence that summarizes the information.

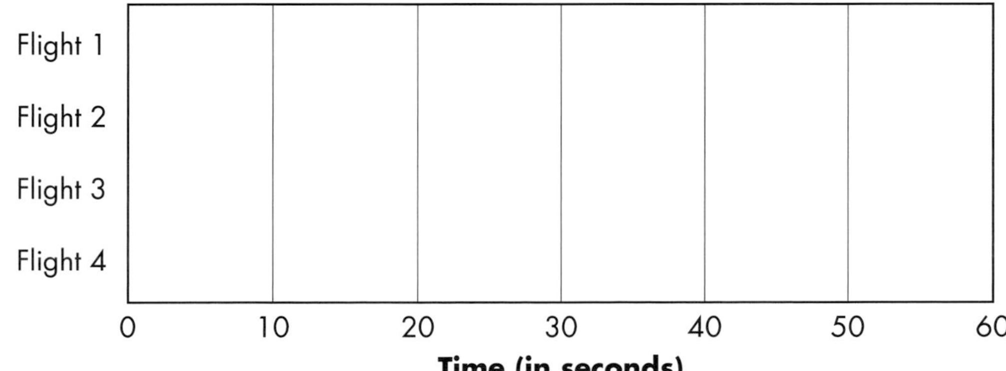

Summary: ______________________________

____

Making Connections

Read the article below. Then answer the questions.

The Queen of Aerobatics

Loops, spins, barrel rolls, knife edges—what do all of these terms have in common? They are all part of the exciting world of aerobatics, thrilling stunts performed in special airplanes.

The word "aerobatics" is a combination of two words, "aero," meaning something relating to airplanes, and "acrobatics." Aerobatics are not for everyone. To become a successful aerobatic pilot, a person must be very brave and skilled, like pilot Patty Wagstaff.

From her very first airplane lesson in 1979, Wagstaff knew she wanted to be a pilot. She enjoyed the thrill of flying so much that she earned licenses to fly five kinds of airplanes and even a helicopter.

Later, Wagstaff joined the USA Aerobatics Team and began to gather experience flying death-defying air routines. In 1991, Wagstaff became the first woman in U.S. history to win the National Aerobatic Championship.

Patty Wagstaff went on to win the championship again for the next two years. Today, she continues to invent and test new aerobatics routines. In 2004, Wagstaff was inducted into the National Aviation Hall of Fame.

Over the last 20 years, Patty Wagstaff has become a pioneer of flight. One of her airplanes is on display in the National Air & Space Museum in Washington, D.C., right next to the airplane of another famous U.S. pilot: Amelia Earhart.

1. In one short sentence, **summarize** the second paragraph of the article.

____

2. **Summarize** the life of Patty Wagstaff.

____

____

____

3. Write a possible heading for the last paragraph of the article.

____

Apply Your Knowledge **Think about the story "Flying to Victory" and the articles you have read in this unit. Answer the questions below.**

Think about the ways flight has changed the world. How do you think flight will develop in the future? What information supports your predictions?

I believe that ____

____

____

____

____

Because ____

____

____

____

____

Choose a Team Project **Choose one of the following group activities, and complete it using your knowledge of flight.**

Flight Exhibit

Discuss the flights you have learned about in this unit. Choose three that you believe are the most important in the history of flight. Think of one object from each of these milestones that you could put in a museum exhibit. Write signs for each object describing what it is and why it is in the exhibit. Share the display with your class.

The Ultimate Airplane

The Airbus A380 is an enormous airplane the length of a football field. Imagine that your group has the chance to decide what to include inside this huge aircraft. Draw a floor plan of the plane's interior with the features you think people would enjoy on a long airplane trip. Summarize your ultimate airplane for the class.

Elephant Safari

Make Inferences in Fiction

Stories don't always tell readers everything. Readers must often use story clues to **make inferences**, or draw conclusions.

To make inferences, readers can combine story clues with information they already know.

- **Story Clue:** *Gita likes to take photographs of city life.*
- **What I Know:** *There is not much wildlife in cities.*
- **Inference:** *Gita probably does not take many wildlife photographs.*

Reader's Guide

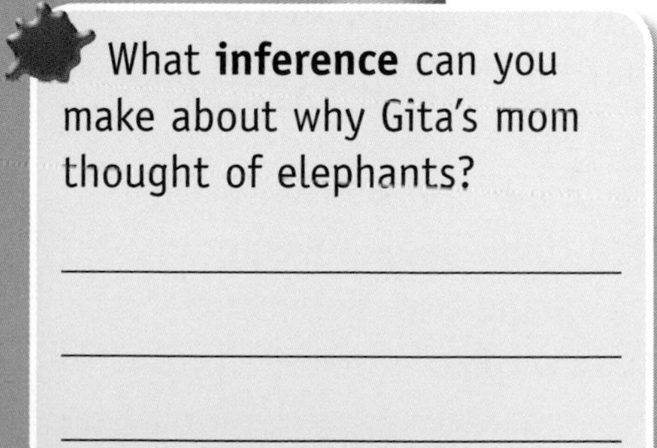

What **inference** can you make about why Gita's mom thought of elephants?

____

____

____

Use the highlighted sentences and the Reader's Guide to make inferences in this story.

"Speaking of elephants," said Gita's mom, stopping at a red light, "would you like to ride one?"

"What? We weren't even talking about elephants," Gita said. Then she noticed the billboard across the street. It was an ad for a car insurance company that showed an elephant stepping on the hood of a car. The slogan read "Accidents Happen."

"Would I like to ride an elephant? That's a strange question," said Gita.

"Some friends offered to take us on an elephant safari when we're in India, and I said yes," said her mom. "It was a wonderful gesture."

"You said YES?" said Gita, straightening up in her seat. Gita was excited about the family's trip to India, but she wanted to photograph the city of Delhi, not ride elephants in the jungle. Gita hoped to take a photo that would win her hometown newspaper's photography contest.

The weeks before the trip passed quickly, and before she knew it, Gita was on a plane to Delhi, trying without success to sleep sitting up. Before they had spent a whole day in India, the entire family piled into a truck and headed outside the city to Corbett National Park. When they arrived at the park, they walked through the gates to wait for their guide.

As Gita waited, she felt an odd sensation move up her back. She jumped, and then spun around to see an elephant's trunk reaching out to her. A large, wrinkly, gray elephant towered over the family. A thin man in a safari hat stepped out of the elephant's shadow and waved. "I'm Mr. Guha," he said, "and this is Winifred. She was just saying hello."

Under Mr. Guha's watchful eye, the family received some quick training in riding elephants. Then each climbed up onto one of the five elephants that stood waiting with handlers. Gita climbed up onto the platform on top of Winifred, and after a few minutes of practice, the group moved along the path and started their safari.

The elephants moved along the path by a stream, swaying through the thick brown grass. Even with her attention focused on not falling off the high platform, Gita grew fascinated with Winifred. The huge animal gently plucked leaves from trees with her trunk, using it like a hand, and she never seemed to get tired.

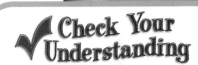

What can you **infer** about Gita from the highlighted paragraph?

____

____

____

Check Your Understanding

Do you:

_ combine story details with what you know to make inferences?

_ make inferences about story characters?

What clues help you **infer** that the family had never ridden elephants before?

1. ______________________

____

2. ______________________

____

When they stopped for lunch, Gita climbed down from her platform and looked at Winifred. The elephant looked at her with kind eyes and gently touched Gita's shoulder with her trunk. Inspired by the elephant's expressions, Gita took several snapshots with her camera, focusing on Winifred's eyes and trunk.

What can you **infer** about the elephant's feelings for Gita?

____

____

____

When the sky reddened with the sunset, the family rode their elephants back to the park entrance. Gita was reluctant to say goodbye to her new friend. After climbing down to the ground, she wrapped her arms around the elephant as best she could, and Winifred wrapped her trunk around Gita in return. Gita had never thought that an animal could be so kind and beautiful. She was glad she had taken pictures of her unforgettable wildlife experience.

Gita spent her last days in India exploring the streets of Delhi and taking more photographs. By the time she stepped back onto the plane to the United States, she felt confident that there was a prize-winning photograph in her collection.

Once she returned, Gita prepared her entry for the city photography contest. She included photos of places in Delhi. Then, just for fun, she added a single photo of Winifred. It wasn't the artistic kind of city photo that Gita usually liked, and it probably wouldn't win, but the photo of Winifred always made her smile.

The contest winners were to be announced in the newspaper the following Sunday. Gita rushed out to get the paper and was surprised to find her picture of Winifred staring at her from the front page under the headline, "Student Photographer Wins Photo Contest." Gita smiled when she thought of all the people who would now have the chance to get to know her friend, the gentle elephant named Winifred.

In what way do people now have the chance to get to know Winifred?

____

____

____

Keep Thinking

Think about the story "Elephant Safari." Circle the letter next to the best answer.

1. What **inference** can you make about elephant trunks?
- **A** Elephants use them only for smelling.
- **B** They are dangerous.
- **C** They are used only for bathing.
- **D** Elephants use them to greet others.

2. Which new title best summarizes the story?
- **A** Gita Takes a New Kind of Picture
- **B** The Bumpy Elephant Ride
- **C** Gita's Voyage Through India
- **D** Accidents Happen

3. Compare and contrast the photos that Gita entered in the contest.
- **A** Most of the photos were from the United States, but one was from India.
- **B** Most of the photos were of Delhi, but one was of Winifred.
- **C** Most of the photos were of Winifred, but one was of Delhi.
- **D** Most of the photos showed wildlife, but one showed people in the city.

Write your answers on the lines.

4. Do you think Gita would want to take another elephant safari? Why or why not?

____

____

____

5. How might Gita's photography change as a result of her winning the contest?

____

____

6. Make an **inference** about a possible reason the photo of Winifred won the contest.

____

____

____

Get Organized

Combine story clues with what you already know to make two **inferences** about the story.

Story Clue
Winifred used her trunk to greet Gita and to pick leaves.

+

What I Know

Inference

Story Clue

+

What I Know

Inference
Gita will probably take more photos of animals.

Summarize

Write a caption to go below Gita's prize-winning photo on the front page of the newspaper. Describe where the photo came from and why it was taken.

Write Away!

Team Up

Work with a partner. Imagine that the story continues, and Gita's interests change completely. She begins to take photos only of animals and nature. Write three story clues that could help readers **infer** that Gita's interests are changing.

1. ______________________________
2. ______________________________
3. ______________________________

On Your Own

Write a sequel to the story that tells about an encounter Gita has with some elephants at the city zoo. Describe the action in the story in a way that lets readers **infer** the characters' feelings.

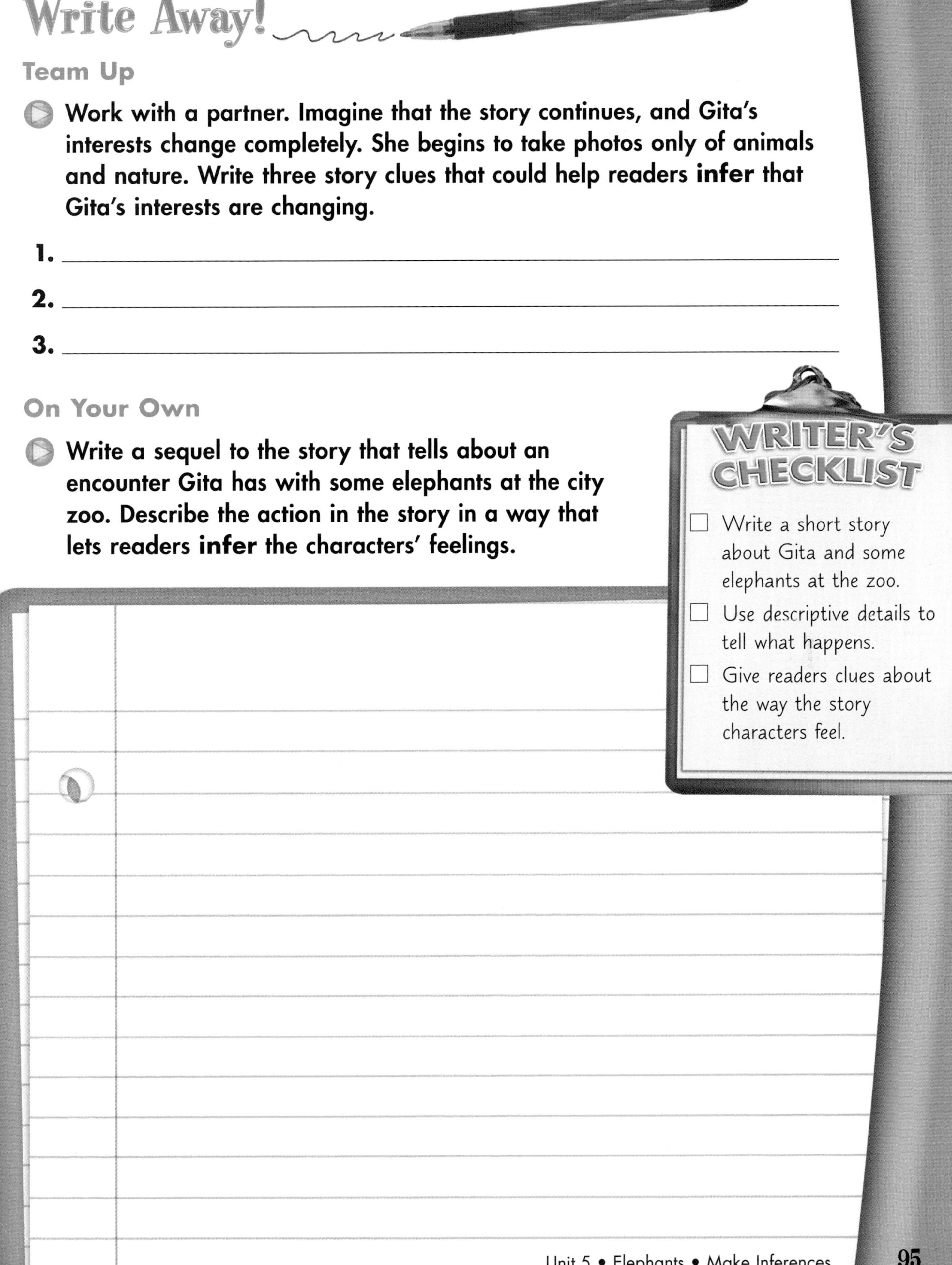

WRITER'S CHECKLIST
☐ Write a short story about Gita and some elephants at the zoo.
☐ Use descriptive details to tell what happens.
☐ Give readers clues about the way the story characters feel.

LESSON 18

MEET THE ELEPHANTS

Make Inferences in Science

When reading science articles, readers must often **make inferences.** Two or more details can be combined to make an inference.

- **Details:** *There are three kinds of elephants. Their ears, tusks, and trunks are unique.*
- **Inference:** *The way to tell different kinds of elephants apart is by looking at their ears, tusks, and trunks.*

Reader's Guide

What two details can help readers **infer** that elephants live in groups?

1. ______________________

____

2. ______________________

____

savanna a flat grassland in a warm area

Use the highlighted sentences and the Reader's Guide to make inferences in this article.

Have you ever seen an elephant in action? The largest land animal in the world is also one of the strongest. Yet these huge beasts are surprisingly gentle. They form social relationships and even communicate with each other. With their unique appearance and behavior, elephants are interesting animals to study.

Three Types of Elephants

Many people don't know that there are actually three types of elephants. Two species of elephants live in Africa: African **savanna** elephants roam dry grasslands, and African forest elephants live in rain forests. The third kind of elephant is found in India and Southeast Asia. Asian elephants live along the edges of tropical rain forests.

The three species of elephants look similar, but their ears, tusks, and trunks are unique. All elephants have large ears, which they flap to cool off. However, both kinds of African elephants have larger ears than Asian elephants. The ears of African forest elephants are more rounded than the ears of African savanna elephants.

Elephants' tusks also can be very different from each other. African savanna elephants have thick, curving tusks. African forest elephants have thin, almost straight tusks that are slightly pinkish in color. Many Asian elephants don't have tusks at all. Elephants that do have tusks use them for digging, lifting, and fighting. Elephants often use one tusk more than the other in the same way that humans prefer their right or left hand.

A trunk is even more useful to an elephant than its tusks. An elephant uses its trunk as a nose for smelling and as an arm for reaching, lifting, bathing, and touching. Elephant trunks are strong enough to lift fallen trees, but they are also gentle enough for an elephant to pick a single leaf! Fingerlike structures on the tip of the trunk allow the elephant to pick up small things. Asian elephants have one "finger," and African elephants have two "fingers."

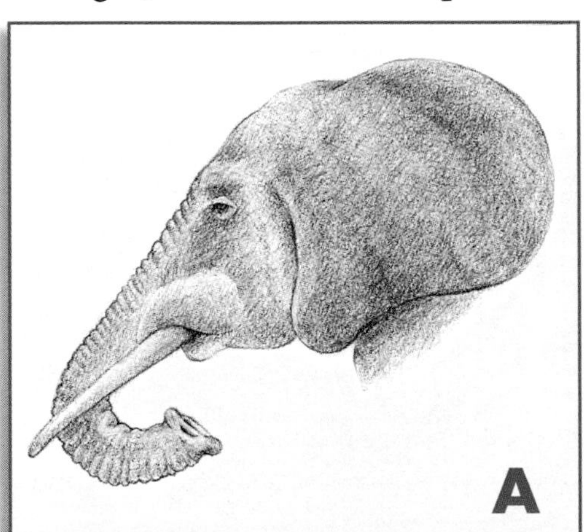

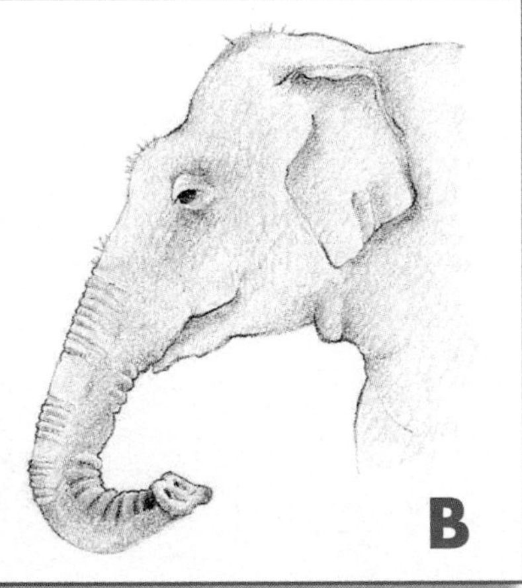

▲ Can you identify each species of elephant?

A: African forest elephant
B: Asian elephant
C: African savanna elephant

What two details about ears can help people **infer** the species of elephant?

1. ______________________

____

2. ______________________

____

From the highlighted details, make an **inference** about what elephants eat.

____

____

____

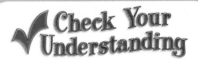

Check Your Understanding

Do you:

__ combine details to make inferences?

__ use diagrams and photos to understand details?

matriarch female leader of a family or community

Make an **inference** about the reason young elephants stay in the family group.

____

____

____

predators animals that hunt other animals for food

Why might an elephant scream loudly and stomp the ground?

____

____

____

Elephant Groups

All three species of elephants form strong social bonds. Adult male elephants live on their own or in a small group of other males, while female elephants live in larger family groups. The family group consists of a **matriarch**, her sisters and daughters, and their calves. As the oldest and wisest member of the family, the matriarch guides the group. She helps them find food and make decisions about when and where to travel.

All of the adult elephants in the family group help care for the calves. If they sense danger, the adults form a circle around the young elephants to protect them. Young elephants stay in their family groups for years. Male elephants usually leave the group at about age twelve, but females stay with the family all their lives.

Elephant Communication

All elephants use sounds and body language to communicate. They use different sounds and behaviors with family members, strangers, and **predators**.

When elephant friends or family members meet after being apart for some time, they have a greeting ceremony. They touch each other with their trunks and make rumbles, squeals, and trumpeting sounds.

▲ Elephants welcome each other with a greeting ceremony.

To threaten a predator, elephants may stomp the ground and flap their ears while screaming loudly. Elephants have specific screams that signal danger to other elephants.

By studying elephants in action, scientists have learned many interesting facts about the types of elephants in the world and the ways they behave. They may be large and powerful, but elephants are actually gentle and caring friends.

Keep Thinking

Think about the article "Meet the Elephants." Circle the letter next to the best answer.

1. What **inference** can you make based on elephants' greeting ceremonies?
   - **A** Elephants use different sounds when the matriarch is nearby.
   - **B** Elephant sounds can be heard from many miles away.
   - **C** Elephants remember other elephants they have met before.
   - **D** Elephants don't like to live in family groups.

2. What is the main idea of the article?
   - **A** Elephants are some of the strongest animals in the world.
   - **B** Different kinds of elephants have different shapes and sizes of tusks.
   - **C** Elephants can communicate with each other.
   - **D** In appearance and behavior, elephants are unique in many ways.

3. Which of the following sentences best contrasts the different kinds of elephants?
   - **A** All elephants have fingers on the ends of their trunks.
   - **B** Each elephant species has unique ears, tusks, and trunks.
   - **C** Many Asian elephants do not have tusks.
   - **D** African forest elephants have pinkish tusks.

Write your answers on the lines.

4. What two details show that elephants use body language to scare off predators?

____

____

5. By looking at an elephant's tusks, how could you **infer** that it uses one tusk more than the other?

____

____

6. Why would the matriarch be the best elephant to guide the family? Explain.

____

____

____

Get Organized

Fill in the chart to make three **inferences** by combining details from the article.

Detail		Detail		Inference
Elephants can lift fallen trees with their trunks.	+		=	Elephants can use their trunks like arms and fingers.
Female elephants live in large family groups.	+	The whole group helps care for young elephants.	=	
Elephants greet other elephants.	+		=	

Summarize

Suppose that you are writing a book about elephants for very young children. Write three or four simple sentences to describe what you know about elephants.

Write Away!

Team Up

Work with a partner. What do you find most fascinating about elephants? Think of four interesting details you have learned about elephants, and list them below.

1. ______________________________
2. ______________________________
3. ______________________________
4. ______________________________

On Your Own

Imagine that you are studying elephants in Africa and writing a report about their social behavior. Describe what you might see, and make **inferences** about why elephants behave the way they do.

WRITER'S CHECKLIST

- ☐ Clearly describe several details of elephant behavior.
- ☐ Include information about elephant groups and communication.
- ☐ Make inferences about why elephants act the way they do.

Make Inferences in Social Studies

Social studies articles often give facts about past events. Readers **make inferences** about the facts to understand how and why things happened.

- **Fact:** *People used to buy many things made from ivory.*
- **Inference:** *People didn't realize that elephants were killed for their ivory.*

Some inferences can be incorrect. As a result, readers must revise their inferences as they learn more information.

Living with Elephants

Reader's Guide

What **inference** can you make from the highlighted details?

____

____

conserve to protect from loss or harm

Use the highlighted sentences and the Reader's Guide to make inferences in this article.

Elephants are thoughtful and sensitive animals. They work together to care for young or sick elephants. They mourn together when an elephant in their family group dies, and they live in peace with most other animals.

Unfortunately, these gentle, intelligent creatures are under threat. They have been hunted almost to extinction for their ivory tusks. They have also been driven out of their natural habitats by growing human populations. People are working to **conserve** the remaining elephant habitats and to protect the elephants in them.

Elephant Habitats

Asian elephants live in Southeast Asia and India, mostly in the tropical rain forests, where their gray color blends into the shadows to hide and protect them. African forest elephants live in the forests of western and central Africa. Asian elephants and African forest elephants feed mainly on the trees and grasses of the forests.

African savanna elephants live in southern and eastern Africa. During the rainy season, African savanna elephants eat the savanna grasses. In drier times, they retreat to the forests for shade and food.

All elephants eat bark, grasses, tree fruits, and leaves. They also visit salt licks to get extra minerals in their diet. An elephant can eat about 145 pounds of food each day! To get this much food, herds need to be able to roam freely over hundreds of miles.

What can you **infer** about the needs of the savanna elephant?

____

____

____

▲ Elephants need a large habitat to find enough food to eat.

Check Your Understanding

Do you:

_ use details to help you make inferences?

_ revise inferences when you learn new information?

Threats to Elephants

Elephants need a great deal of space to roam and eat. They once ranged all over Africa and Asia. In the 20th century, however, human populations grew rapidly. Towns and cities sprang up where there used to be only forests and grasslands. The paths elephants took were suddenly full of people, cities, and farms.

Elephants could destroy homes and farms just by walking on their usual paths. As a result, elephants that came near people began to be killed or frightened away. Large herds of elephants were crowded into smaller areas, which led to smaller herds.

Complete the chart with details that support the following **inference**.

Inference
People and elephants did not always get along.
Supporting Details
1. ______________________
2. ______________________

poaching the illegal hunting of animals

ban a law making an activity illegal

Make an **inference** about why there was a ban on ivory.

___

___

___

How might refusing to buy ivory help the elephant population?

___

___

___

The loss of needed habitat has been a large threat to elephant survival. However, the illegal hunting of elephants known as **poaching** has done the most damage to elephants in the wild. Poachers kill elephants just to get their valuable ivory tusks. In fact, from 1979 to 1989, poachers killed nearly half of the African elephant population.

Helping Elephants Survive

Even though elephants are still under threat, it is not too late to help them survive. People around the world are working to preserve the elephant population and to create more protected areas for them.

One of the main concerns of lawmakers is to find ways to stop poaching. About 15 years ago, an international **ban** on ivory was passed. Today, it is still illegal to buy or sell ivory from threatened elephant populations. Lawmakers hope that this will stop poachers from killing elephants.

Elephant populations are still declining, but they can be saved. More people are learning ways to help elephants. Whether they are conserving elephant habitats or refusing to buy ivory, millions of people around the world are committed to keeping these incredible animals safe.

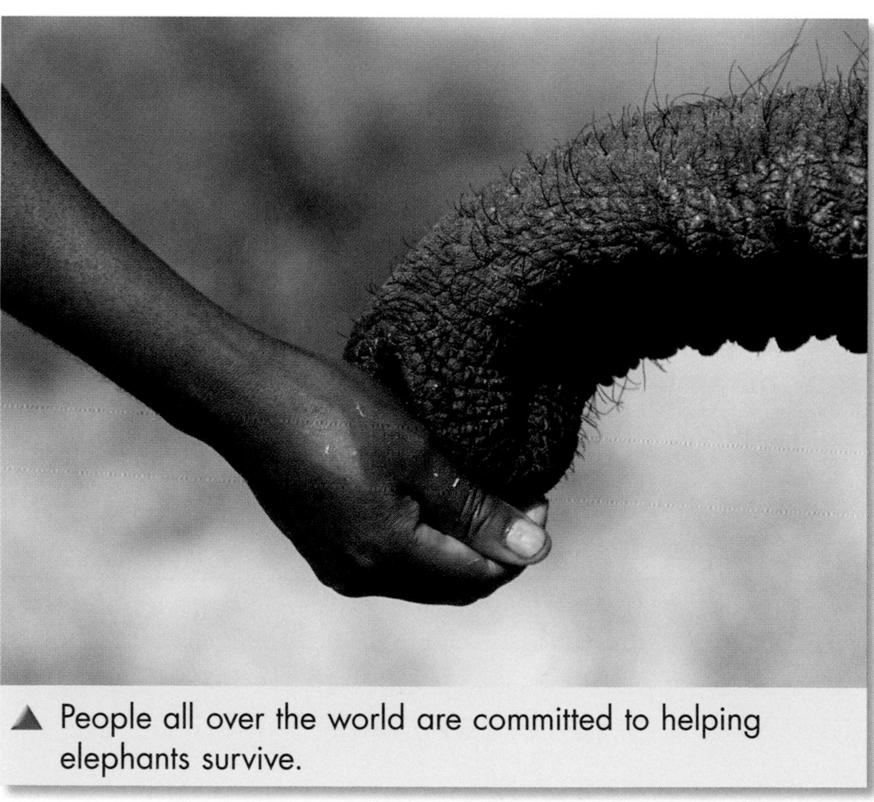

▲ People all over the world are committed to helping elephants survive.

Keep Thinking

Think about the article "Living with Elephants." Circle the letter next to the best answer.

1. What can you **infer** is the greatest threat to elephants?
   - **A** other animals
   - **B** loss of habitat
   - **C** lawmakers
   - **D** humans

2. What do all African and Asian elephants have in common?
   - **A** Their tusks are made of ivory.
   - **B** They live in Asia.
   - **C** They live in forests in the rainy season.
   - **D** They eat savanna grasses.

3. Why was an international ban on ivory passed?
   - **A** to stop the loss of elephant habitat
   - **B** to make people want to buy and sell ivory
   - **C** to stop poachers from hunting elephants for their ivory
   - **D** to protect the areas where elephants lived

Write your answers on the lines.

4. From the highlighted detail, what can you **infer** about the climate in southern Africa?

   During the rainy season, African savanna elephants eat the savanna grasses. In drier times, they retreat to the forests for shade and food.

   ____

   ____

5. Why do you think people want to help elephants?

   ____

   ____

6. What **inference** can you make about the ivory ban? Is it working to save the elephant population?

   ____

   ____

Get Organized

Combine the three details from the article to make two inferences about what will happen to elephants in the future.

Detail

Elephant habitats are shrinking as human populations grow.

1. ____________________

2. ____________________

Detail

Poachers killed nearly half of all African elephants between 1979 and 1989.

Detail

Many people are working to protect elephant populations and stop the ivory trade.

Summarize

Imagine that you are giving a speech to your classmates about why elephant populations are endangered. Write a short speech describing threats to elephants and what is being done about them.

____

____

____

____

Write Away!

Team Up

Work with a partner. Discuss two other ways that people could help elephants. Make **inferences** about the effects that the actions would have.

1. ____

____

2. ____

____

On Your Own

Imagine that the year is 2025, and elephants are finally safe. Write an essay explaining how you think this happened. Make **inferences** about the actions people must have taken to solve the problems that elephants faced before 2025.

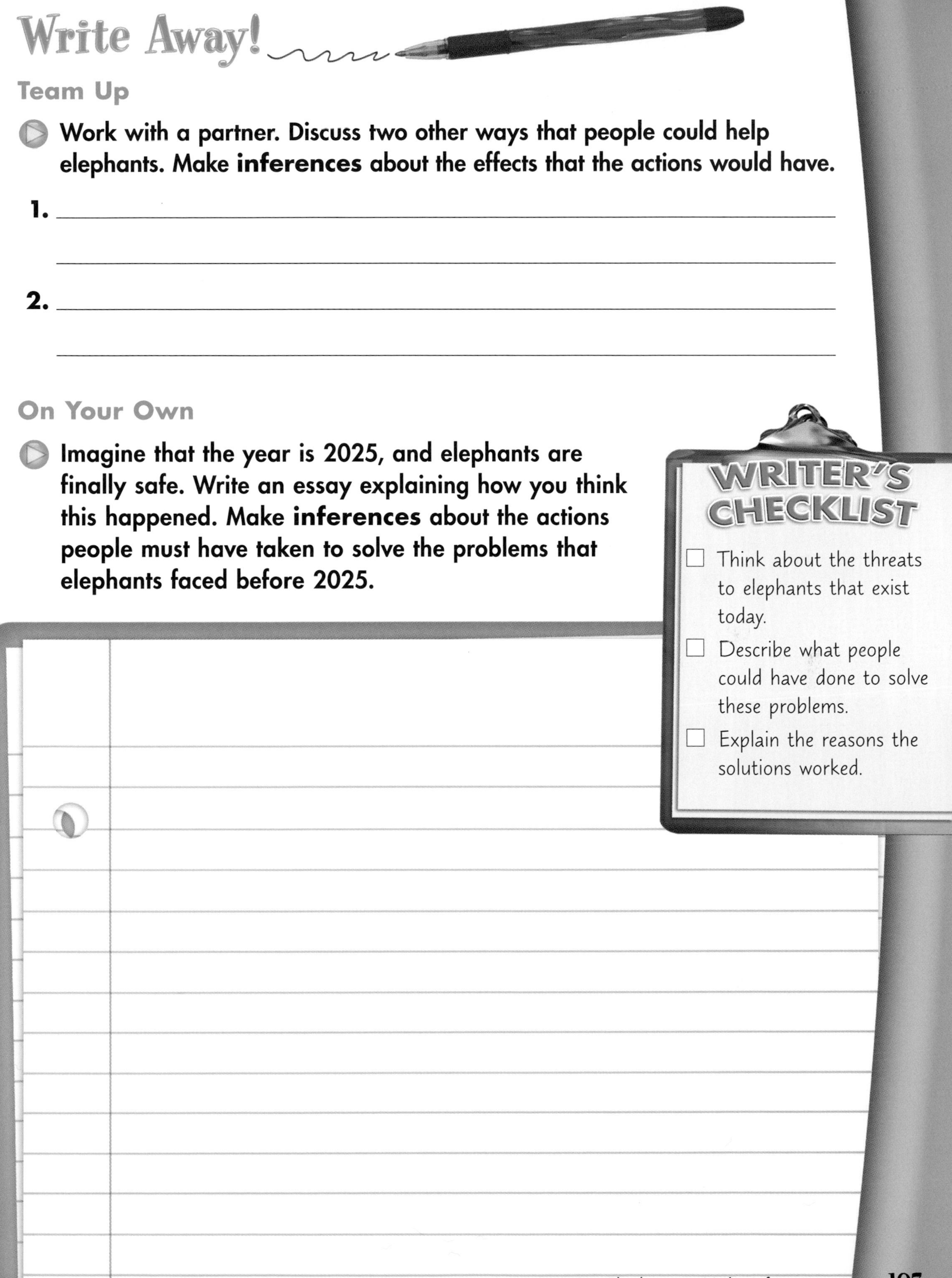

WRITER'S CHECKLIST
☐ Think about the threats to elephants that exist today.
☐ Describe what people could have done to solve these problems.
☐ Explain the reasons the solutions worked.

LESSON 20

Make Inferences in Math

In math, the numbers on a chart or graph usually represent facts. Thinking about these facts together can help readers **make inferences**.

- **Fact:** *In 1900, there were about 10 million African elephants.*
- **Fact:** *In 1979, there were only about 1.3 million African elephants.*
- **Inference:** *Something must have happened to cause this major drop in number.*

Gather Information **The elephant population in Africa has been falling for many reasons. Study the chart below that shows the changes over time.**

The Elephant Population in Africa

Year	Population
1979	1,300,000
1989	620,000
1995	579,532
1998	487,345
2002	420,000

Understand a Line Graph

A line graph can make it easier to see the way the elephant population has changed over time. Study the line graph. Then use the line graph and the chart to answer the questions.

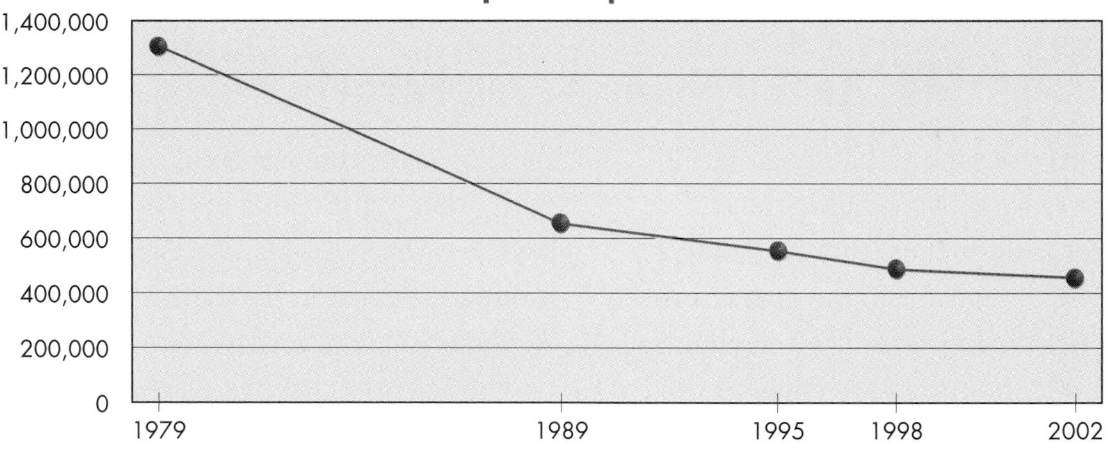

1. Between which years did the greatest drop in population occur? By about how much?

____

2. Between which years was the smallest drop? What could account for this?

____

____

3. From the line graph, what can you **infer** about the future elephant population?

____

____

Make Your Own Line Graph

In some African countries, efforts to help elephants have been successful, and the elephant population is rising. Fill in the line graph below for elephants in South Africa.

The Elephant Population in South Africa

Year	Population
1979	8,000
1991	8,200
1998	11,900

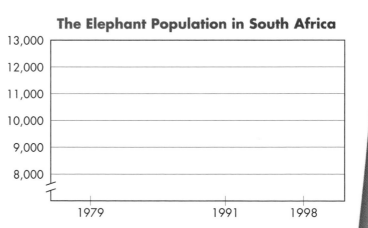

The Elephant Population in South Africa

13,000
12,000
11,000
10,000
9,000
8,000

1979 1991 1998

Making Connections

Read the article below. Then answer the questions.

An Elephant Never Forgets

There is an old saying that goes, "an elephant never forgets." What is the source of this saying, and is there any truth to it?

The saying dates back many years to the time when people first observed elephants in the wild. Elephants always traveled the same routes from place to place, and they seemed to remember every twist and turn on their journey, even after not having made it for years.

One scientist created a test to find out if there was any scientific evidence to support the saying about an elephant's memory. He took two boxes and marked one with a picture of a square and one with a picture of a circle. Then he filled the box marked with a square with food.

It took the elephant 330 tries to understand the idea that the box marked with the square always held the food. The scientist then tried putting the food in boxes marked with other symbols. Every time the scientist switched the symbols, the elephant figured it out a little faster. By the 20th time, the elephant knew exactly what to do.

The scientist discovered that an elephant can learn, but what he really wondered was how long it would remember. He waited for a whole year and tried the experiment again with the same elephant and the same symbols. On all except one try, the elephant chose successfully—it had remembered!

This experiment shows that it might take a long time to teach an elephant, but once it learns something, it doesn't soon forget it!

1. What two details support the **inference** that once an elephant learns, it remembers?

____

____

2. What can you **infer** from the number of tries needed for an elephant to learn?

____

3. Is it a correct **inference** to say that elephants never forget? Explain your answer.

____

____

Apply Your Knowledge **Think about the story "Elephant Safari" and the articles you have read in this unit. Answer the questions below.**

Based on what you know, make an **inference** about the future of elephants, and write a few sentences about the way you came to your conclusion.

____

____

____

____

If you could have any job helping elephants, what would it be? Explain the reasons you would want this job.

____

____

____

____

Choose a Team Project **Choose one of the following group activities, and complete it using your knowledge of elephants.**

Interview with an Elephant

Elephants can live to be 60 years old and are known for their long memories. If an elephant could talk, what do you think it would say about its life and what it has seen? With your group, write a fictional interview with a very old elephant. Have each member of the group ask at least two questions. Then work together with the rest of the group to answer the questions. Read your finished interview to the class.

Elephant Park

Suppose that your group has been chosen to create a new park where elephants will be protected. In your group, discuss what you know about elephants, and then decide what they would need to live a comfortable life. Make a list of the features your new park would offer and why each one is important to elephants. Then write a press release that announces the park to the public, and read it to the class.

LESSON 21

SAVE EVERY SPORT!

Fact and Opinion in Fiction

A **fact** tells something that is true and can be proven. An **opinion** tells what a person feels or believes.

- **Fact:** *The school board voted to cut sports funding.*
- **Opinion:** *The students believe it is wrong to cut funding for school activities.*

Opinion clue words, such as *feel, think,* and *believe,* often help readers identify an opinion.

Reader's Guide

List one **fact** and one **opinion** from the highlighted sentences.

Fact: ____________________

____

Opinion: ____________________

____

Use the highlighted sentences and the Reader's Guide to identify facts and opinions in this story.

Luis stood at the fax machine reading the most recent message, which had the subject "Sports" written at the top. He stood perfectly still, except for scratching his chin, which he did whenever he concentrated. Shayla stopped typing and leaned back in her chair, rubbing her tired fingers. "I haven't seen that look on your face since you uncovered the news that the class election was rigged," she said.

Luis and Shayla were the two best writers on the staff of their school newspaper, *The Lantern*. Luis wrote a column called "Hear Me Out!" in which he voiced his opinions on school events. Shayla wrote articles about local issues, such as the discovery that a company was dumping chemicals into the river near their school.

Luis handed Shayla the fax. "Just read it," he said.

"School board approves budget cuts in the area of athletics," she read aloud. "Wait," she said suddenly, "It says here that they are going to cut two school sports."

"It looks like we've got work to do," said Luis.

Later that morning when Katie Davis, captain of the girls' volleyball team, left the locker room after gym class, Luis was waiting with pencil in hand.

"You're here about the budget cuts, aren't you?" asked Katie. "Tell me what you know," she said.

"Only one thing," Luis said, "that football is not going to be cut."

"Of course not," Katie said, rolling her eyes. "The school board would never cut football. They'll choose some smaller sport like volleyball. This is so unfair." Luis wrote as fast as he could to keep up with Katie's remarks:

"I may not be the best student in the world," says volleyball captain, Katie Davis, "but I do know one thing—I am good at sports. Volleyball may not bring in the most fans or make a lot of money, but it gives the girls on the team confidence, and it's worth saving for that reason alone."

After school, Shayla walked past the neighborhood park and saw the athlete she was looking for right away—he was hard to miss. Tommy Shot, the school basketball star, was six feet, seven inches tall! He spent his evenings coaching youth basketball.

"Tommy!" she called, hurrying across the park and taking out her tape recorder. "Have you heard about the budget cuts?"

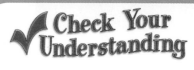

Check Your Understanding

Do you:

__ look for facts and opinions as you read?

__ think about the opinions of different characters?

What is one of Katie's **opinions** in the highlighted paragraph?

____

____

____

Underline three **facts** about Tommy Shot.

"Sure have," said Tommy. "It's awful." As Tommy went on, Shayla recorded what he said:

"I don't think the school should have to cut any sports. It is like asking parents to pick their favorite child—I don't feel that anyone should have to make a decision like that!"

Write two clue words that show readers that Tommy Shot is expressing an **opinion**.

____

____

Luis and Shayla spent the next two days interviewing students. After ten interviews, it became clear to them that cutting any sport was a terrible idea. The two reporters spent the weekend in the newsroom, writing an article together for the front page of the school newspaper. They called their article "Save Every Sport!"

The Lantern

SAVE EVERY SPORT!

The special issue of *The Lantern* came out first thing Monday morning, and every copy was gone from the school newsstand by noon. The newspaper staff spent the afternoon making extra copies and delivering them to local libraries, coffee shops, and convenience stores.

Almost as soon as the newspaper came out, Luis and Shayla's article drew media attention. It was featured on the local news, which motivated parents to call the school board and voice their opinions. Before the end of the week, the school board had called an emergency session and voted to approve more funding for the school's sports programs.

How did **opinions** make a difference in the highlighted paragraph?

____

____

____

____

Despite their huge success, Luis and Shayla were back in the newsroom the next day. It was just like any other day at *The Lantern,* only now they had decided to write a new weekly column together. They called it "The Power of the Press."

Keep Thinking

Think about the story "Save Every Sport!" Circle the letter next to the best answer.

1. In their article, Luis and Shayla expressed their **opinion** that
- **A** sports were not as important as everyone thought they were.
- **B** the school board should not cut any school sports.
- **C** football was the most important sport at the school.
- **D** writing an article about sports would make them popular.

2. What inference can readers make about the **opinions** of the parents in the story?
- **A** Parents didn't think that school reporters should cover that kind of news.
- **B** Parents believed that only the less popular school sports should be saved.
- **C** Parents thought it was fine to cut some sports but not others.
- **D** Parents believed that it was wrong to cut any of the school's sports.

3. What other title would best summarize Luis and Shayla's article?
- **A** "Tommy Shot: Basketball Star"
- **B** "Girls' Volleyball Must Stay"
- **C** "The Cut That Hurts Everyone"
- **D** "Why Sports Don't Matter"

Write your answers on the lines.

4. Write two **facts** about the character Luis.

____

____

5. Which part of the following statement is a **fact**, and which is an **opinion**?

After ten interviews, it became clear to them that cutting any sport was a terrible idea.

____

____

6. What is your **opinion** about the school board's decision to vote again? Use an opinion clue word in your answer.

____

____

____

Get Organized

Fill in the boxes with **facts** about the characters below and their **opinions** from the story.

Characters	Facts	Opinions
Luis and Shayla	1. wrote for the school newspaper 2.	1. believed that an article might help save school sports 2.
Katie Davis	1. 2.	1. 2.
Tommy Shot	1. 2.	1. 2.

Summarize

Imagine that you are a reporter for a city newspaper in Luis and Shayla's town. Write a short article about what they did to save the school's sports.

Write Away!

Team Up

Work with a partner. Suppose that you are being interviewed about the possibility of cutting two sports at your school. Write your **opinion** below, and support it with at least one **fact**.

On Your Own

Imagine that you read Luis and Shayla's article. Write a letter to the newspaper's editors explaining your **opinion** about why two school sports should or should not be cut. Support your opinion with **facts**.

WRITER'S CHECKLIST

- ☐ Write a formal letter.
- ☐ Clearly explain your opinion.
- ☐ Support your opinion with facts.
- ☐ Use clue words to make your opinion clear.

SPEEDY SPORTS

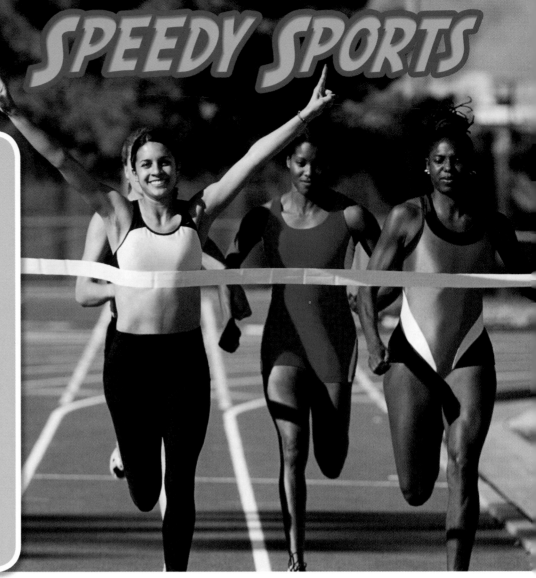

Fact and Opinion in Science

A **fact** is information that can be proven true. An **opinion** is based on a person's ideas or beliefs and cannot be proven true.

- **Fact:** *Athletes are always setting new records in speed.*
- **Opinion:** *Without speed, sports would not be very exciting.*

Science writers often draw conclusions based on facts. These conclusions can be facts or opinions.

Reader's Guide

What is one **fact** about athletes?

___

___

excel to do better

Use the highlighted sentences and the Reader's Guide to identify facts and opinions in this article.

From runners and bicyclists to swimmers and pitchers, athletes show amazing speeds at sporting events. Athletes move, sports machines work, and sports equipment travels at increasingly fast speeds. Athletes are constantly setting new records, which keeps athletes motivated to **excel** and spectators eager to watch. Without speed, sports would not be as exciting.

On Land and in Water

The speed of women and men in water and on land has significantly increased throughout history. Swimmers and runners alike work extremely hard to become stronger. This strength allows them to travel at record-breaking speeds.

At just under one mile in distance, the 1500-meter race is one of the most common events in both swimming and running. Male swimmers have completed the race in less than 15 minutes, which is almost 4 miles per hour (mph). In a much shorter race, the 50-meter sprint, records have been set at 5.5 mph.

Although people have opinions about which is more exciting to watch, athletes on land can move quicker than athletes in water. Racing around the track four times, runners complete the 1500-meter race at remarkably quick paces. The women's record is 3 minutes, 59 seconds—14 mph! The 50-meter sprint has been completed at a rate of 19 mph.

Write one **fact** from the paragraph that supports the highlighted conclusion.

____

____

The Power of Machines

Humans move quickly on land and in water, but human-powered machines move even faster. Sports such as wheelchair racing and cycling have become very **competitive**. These machines travel at extraordinary rates.

competitive the result of many people competing

Since the mid-1940s, wheelchair sports have become extremely exciting sports to watch. Tennis, track, and basketball are among the sports that include athletes in wheelchairs. Wheelchair participants also compete in major marathons. The 26.2-mile race has been completed by a wheelchair athlete in 1 hour and 20 minutes. That is 19.6 mph!

Underline one **opinion** in the highlighted paragraph.

▲ Sports wheelchairs allow athletes to participate in a variety of sports.

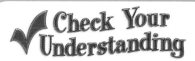

Check Your Understanding

Do you:

_ look for facts that support conclusions?

_ use your own opinions to make connections?

Write one **fact** that supports the highlighted conclusion.

____

____

Bicycles can also travel long distances at amazing speeds. Athletes compete in short bicycle races of just one-half mile to extremely long races that cover 2,000 miles. The bicycles' speeds vary based on the distance and terrain of the race. Records have been set, however, with bikes traveling almost 167 mph.

Flying Objects

In some sports, athletes propel the equipment at amazing speeds. It is hard to imagine, for example, an exciting hockey game with a slow-moving puck.

exertion using strong physical effort

Baseball is one of America's most popular sports, and the speeds at which baseballs are thrown are astonishing. Pitchers can throw a ball with such **exertion** that a batter will hardly even see it coming. Most major-league pitches travel at speeds of more than 65 mph. However, there have been pitches recorded at over 100 mph.

What **facts** support the writer's **opinion** that the speeds of pitches are astonishing?

1. ______________________________

____

____

2. ______________________________

____

____

Speed is also important in the game of tennis. The fastest serve of a tennis ball moved at a rate of 163.6 mph. The all-time fastest serve in sports was a badminton serve that traveled at 199 mph!

Athletes in a variety of sports move at incredible speeds. Some athletes, such as swimmers and runners, travel on their own. Athletes in wheelchairs and on bicycles rely on machines for speed. Others, such as baseball players and tennis players, must react to the quick movement of the equipment used in their sports. Whatever their sport may be, athletes have continued to push themselves to achieve the fastest speeds.

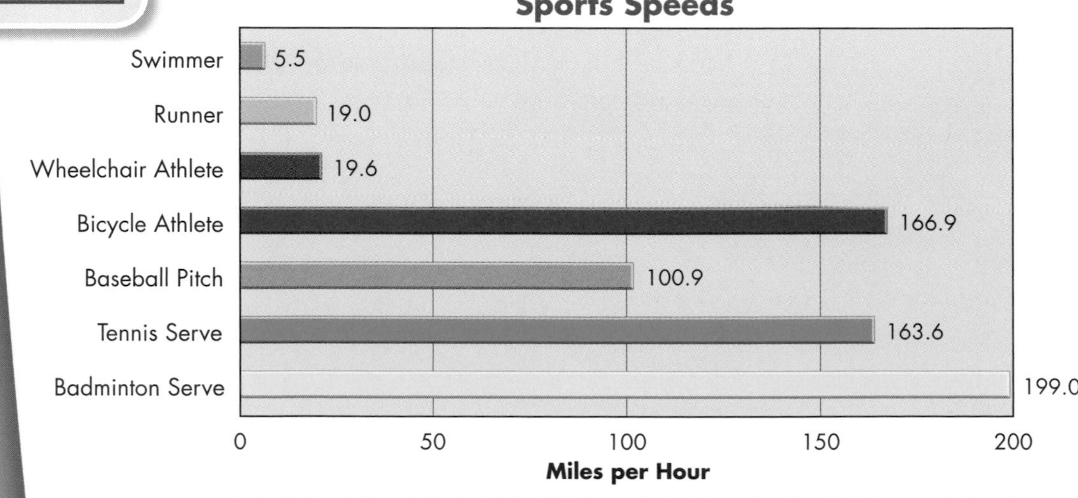

▲ Athletes of all types move at remarkable speeds.

Keep Thinking

Think about the article "Speedy Sports." Circle the letter next to the best answer.

1. Which of the following statements is an **opinion** from the article?
- **A** Athletes can travel faster on land than on water.
- **B** Tennis, track, and basketball are sports that include athletes in wheelchairs.
- **C** Wheelchair sports have become extremely exciting sports to watch.
- **D** Most major-league pitches travel at speeds of more than 65 miles per hour.

2. What is the main idea of the article?
- **A** Bicycles can travel long distances at amazing speeds.
- **B** Many sports are fast because of the equipment used.
- **C** People like to watch sports because of their speed.
- **D** Athletes in a variety of sports move at incredible speeds.

3. The speed of a baseball pitch is mostly due to the
- **A** exertion of the pitcher.
- **B** size of the ball.
- **C** eyesight of the batter.
- **D** spectators and fans.

Write your answers on the lines.

4. What **facts** support the conclusion that athletes can travel faster on land than they can in water?

____

____

5. What information could be given to support the writer's conclusion that baseball is one of the most popular sports in the United States?

____

____

6. What **fact** could support the **opinion** that badminton is the fastest sport?

____

____

Get Organized

Fill in the chart by supporting the writer's conclusions with facts from the article.

Writer's Conclusions	Facts
Athletes on land can move quicker than athletes in water.	The fastest swimming record was 5.5 mph.
Human-powered machines travel at extraordinary rates.	
In some sports, athletes propel the equipment at amazing speeds.	

Summarize

Imagine that you are a news anchor giving a report on the speed of sports. Include facts from several different sports.

Write Away!

Team Up

Work with a partner. Interview each other about the sports you like, and answer the questions below. Record your answers and your partner's answers in the chart.

	Which sport would you like to be really good at?	List a reason why you chose that sport.
Me		
My Partner		

On Your Own

Imagine that you just broke a speed record in the sport you chose above. Reporters are there to interview you. Describe what you did to prepare, give **facts** about your performance, and state your **opinions** about your future in sports.

WRITER'S CHECKLIST

- ☐ Describe the way you trained or prepared.
- ☐ Give facts about what you did.
- ☐ Give your opinions about what you will achieve in the future.

LESSON 23

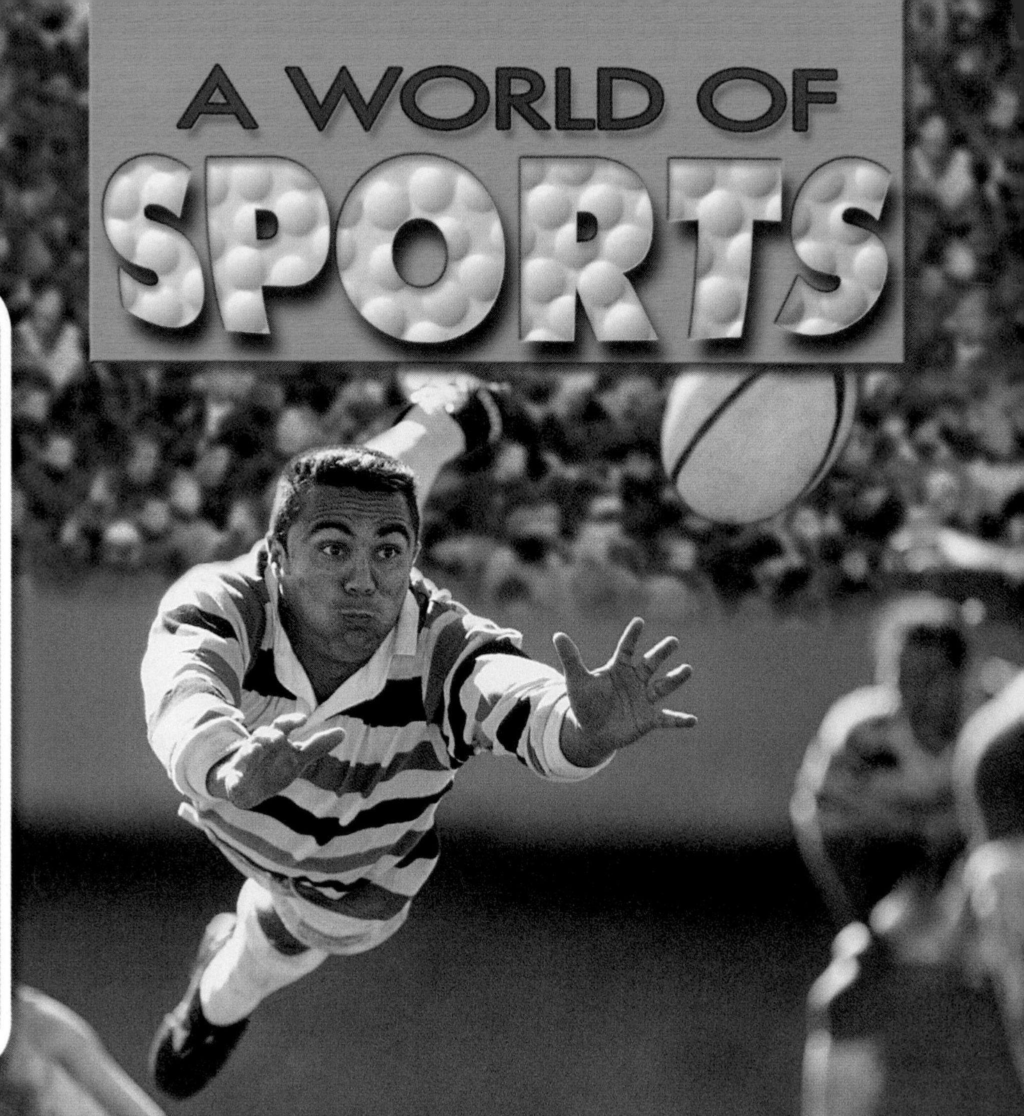

Fact and Opinion in Social Studies

Social studies articles sometimes include both **facts** and **opinions**. Facts can be proven true, but opinions cannot. However, a person can use facts to support an opinion.

- **Opinion:** *Soccer is the world's favorite sport.*
- **Supporting Fact:** *Over 240 million people in more than 200 countries regularly play soccer.*

Reader's Guide

Use the highlighted sentences and the Reader's Guide to identify facts and opinions in this article.

Write one **opinion** from the highlighted paragraph.

____

____

cultural heritage traditions shared by a group of people

It's a beautiful morning. You and your friends are on your way to the park for a game of baseball. Halfway around the world, a different group of students is finishing a game, but it is rugby, not baseball. All over the world, people play sports that are part of their **cultural heritage**.

A sport that is central to the culture of a country is considered a national pastime. Widely played or watched, the game either has a long tradition in the country or has gained recent popularity.

In some countries, the government decides which sport is the national pastime. In other countries, a sport that has had a long history is often regarded as a national pastime, such as baseball in the United States.

New Zealand—In the sport of rugby, players carry a ball in their hands or arms. They can pass it backwards, or sideways, or they can kick it in any direction. New Zealand's national team is the most talented rugby team in history. No other international team has beaten New Zealand's record. However, they are most known worldwide for performing a traditional dance before each international match.

What **fact** supports the highlighted **opinion**?

___

___

___

Thailand—Muay Thai, or Thai boxing, is a form of **martial art** practiced in Southeast Asia. Players face off in a ring. Wearing special gloves, they use kicks and punches against their opponent. Muay Thai is known as the "Science of Eight Limbs" because it requires the use of hands, feet, elbows, and knees.

martial art a type of self-defense often practiced as a sport

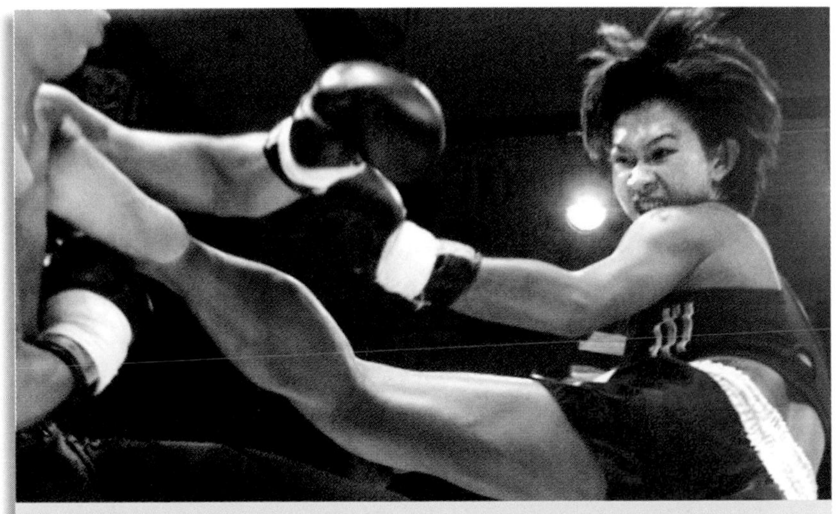

▲ Muay Thai is a martial art that started in Thailand.

Check Your Understanding

Do you:

_ look for facts that support opinions?

_ review photos to understand facts?

Sweden—Like other sports, a game of ice hockey requires equipment and strong players. But the most important element to this sport is the long stretch of ice. Players race across the ice, balanced on the blades of ice skates. Using long sticks, they try to hit a small puck into the opposing team's goal. Long winters and cold temperatures make ice hockey a perfect fit as Sweden's national pastime.

Why does the writer think ice hockey is the perfect national pastime for Sweden?

___

___

___

Venezuela—Baseball, considered the national pastime of the United States, is also wildly loved in Venezuela. In fact, some of the world's best baseball players come from Venezuela. Many athletes from Venezuela have come to the United States to play at the highest level of professional baseball in the world, Major League Baseball.

competitor an opponent or rival

Underline the highlighted sentence that states a **fact**.

What **facts** support the **opinion** that soccer is the greatest team sport?

1. ______________________

____

____

2. ______________________

____

____

Canada—In lacrosse, players use sticks with nets on the end to throw a small rubber ball into a **competitor's** goal. The sport has roots in Native American culture, and its name means "little war." Traditionally, the lacrosse field stretched across three to ten miles, and one game could last for days. Today, lacrosse is popular throughout North America, but the playing field and game lengths are shorter.

Egypt—If you were to visit Egypt, you would see much more than pyramids. You would enjoy watching people playing soccer, which is called football in Egypt and many other countries. Played almost entirely with the feet, players may use any part of their body except their hands and arms to move the ball. Egypt's national football team, nicknamed *The Pharaohs,* was the first African team to compete in the World Cup, which decides the best soccer team in the world.

Over 240 million people in more than 200 countries regularly play soccer. Millions more attend or watch soccer games on television. Simple rules and equipment have helped its popularity grow. Some consider it the greatest team sport in the world. One might say it is the *international* pastime.

▲ Soccer is one of the most popular sports in the world.

National pastimes are as varied as the people who play them and the places in which they are played. Often a country's pastime reflects the culture or geography of the country, such as ice hockey in Sweden. Some sports, like soccer, have developed a more global appeal. Sports are important because they provide a way for people of the world to come together in friendly competition. They let us see what we have in common, as well as what makes us unique.

Keep Thinking

Think about the article "A World of Sports." Circle the letter next to the best answer.

1. Which sentence states an **opinion**?
- **A** Muay Thai is known as the "Science of Eight Limbs."
- **B** Sports are important because they bring people together.
- **C** The word lacrosse means "little war."
- **D** Egypt's national football team is nicknamed *The Pharaohs*.

2. How is the current game of lacrosse different from the traditional game?
- **A** The players now use sticks with nets on the end.
- **B** Lacrosse now means "big war."
- **C** It is now played in North America.
- **D** The playing field and game lengths are now shorter.

3. Which sentence best summarizes the article?
- **A** Sports are part of the cultural heritage of many countries.
- **B** Soccer is the most popular sport in the world.
- **C** Over 240 million people regularly play soccer.
- **D** Baseball is the national pastime of the United States.

Write your answers on the lines.

4. What is one of the writer's **opinions** of national pastimes?

____

____

5. Write a **fact** that supports the following **opinion**:

Venezuela is quickly producing some of the world's best baseball players.

____

____

____

6. Write one **fact** and one **opinion** about soccer from the article.

____

____

____

Get Organized

Fill in the chart to show one **fact** and one **opinion** about the national pastime of each country.

Country	Fact	Opinion
New Zealand	No other rugby team has beaten New Zealand's record.	
Sweden		
Venezuela		

Summarize

Imagine that you have just returned from a trip around the world. You saw people playing many different sports in many different countries. Write a short postcard to your best friend summarizing what you learned about sports around the world.

Write Away!

Team Up

Discuss your favorite sports with a partner. Then choose one sport, and give two **facts** and two **opinions** about it.

Sport: ______________________________

Facts: ______________________________

____

Opinions: ______________________________

____

On Your Own

Imagine that you are a sports writer from another country who is visiting the U.S. Write a short article describing a sport that is common in the U.S. but unknown in your country. Give **facts** about the sport, as well as your **opinions**.

WRITER'S CHECKLIST

- ☐ Write as if you had never seen the sport before.
- ☐ Use facts to describe the sport.
- ☐ Write your opinions about the sport.
- ☐ Support your opinions with facts.

LESSON 24

Ski Jumping

Fact and Opinion in Math

Some sports determine winners based only on **facts**, such as points in a game. Others use a combination of facts and **opinions** to determine who wins. In ski jumping, judges award points based on both facts and opinions.

- *Some points are based on the distance of the jump, a* ***fact*** *that can be proven.*
- *Some points are based on the judges'* ***opinions*** *of the skier's technique, which cannot be proven.*

Gather Information **Each athlete below completed two ski jumps. The chart shows the distance of each jump. It also records the total number of points the judges awarded each athlete's performance, based on both distance and technique.**

Women's Ski Jumping Results

Rank	Competitor	Jump 1 Distance	Jump 2 Distance	Total Points
1	Van, Lindsay	289 feet	335 feet	152.6
2	Jerome, Jessica	285 feet	323 feet	142.4
3	Johnson, Alissa	277 feet	297 feet	121.6

Understand a Bar Graph

A bar graph can help readers compare the distances each athlete jumped. Study the bar graph. Then use the graph and the chart to answer the questions.

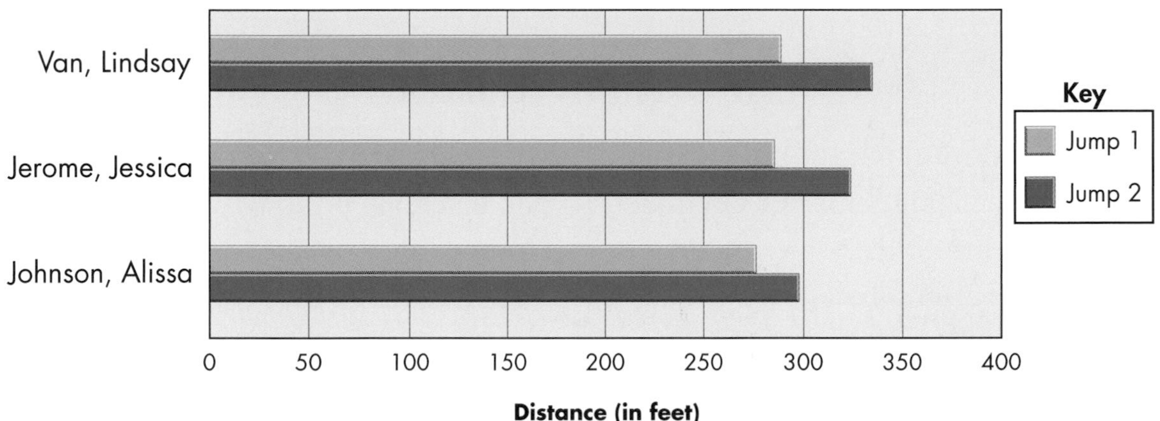

1. What pattern do you notice about each competitor's first and second jumps?

____

2. How can you tell on the graph which line represents each jump?

____

3. Which column in the chart includes the judges' **opinions**?

____

Make Your Own Bar Graph

Use the total points information from the chart to complete the bar graph below. Then give one fact and one opinion about the information.

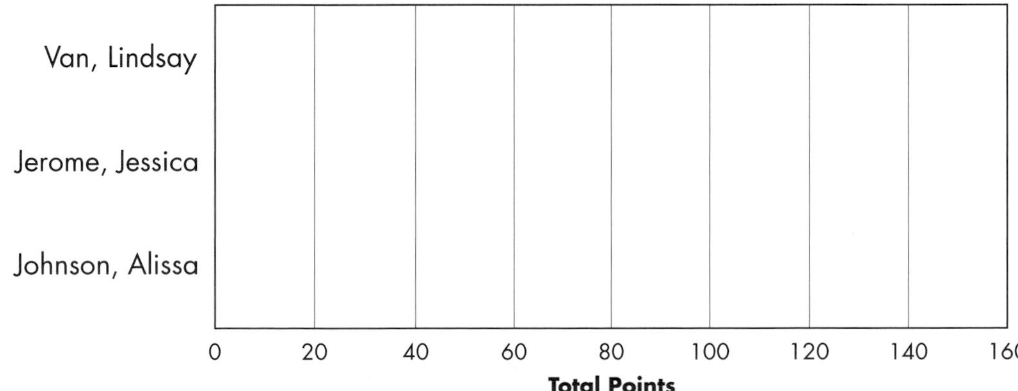

Fact: ____

Opinion: ____

Making Connections

Read the article below. Then answer the questions.

An Olympic Debate

It was the third round of the gymnastics competition at the 2004 Summer Olympic Games. Paul Hamm of the United States was in 12th place after a bad fall. No one thought he had a chance at any medal.

Then, some of the other gymnasts began making serious mistakes. After that, Hamm performed well on the parallel bars event. A high score of 9.837 on his final routine put Hamm in first place.

When the competition ended, Hamm had won the all-around gymnastics gold medal by only .012 points, making it the closest win in Olympic gymnastics history. However, some said he never deserved to win.

Within days of Hamm's win, the International Gymnastics Federation said that the Olympic judges had made a mistake in judging. They said that the judges had wrongly taken points away from a South Korean gymnast named Yang Tae Young, who had gone on to win the bronze medal. This scoring mistake meant that Young should have won the gold medal, not Hamm.

Some people suggested that Hamm should give his gold medal to the other athlete. Others believed that once the medals were awarded, judges should not change their minds.

Many Hamm supporters reviewed the routines and found moments where Young made a different mistake. This meant Hamm still should have won.

The debate went on for months. In the end, Paul Hamm was declared the official winner.

1. What was the **opinion** of the International Gymnastics Federation?

____

2. What are two **facts** about Paul Hamm's Olympic performance?

____

____

3. Write your **opinion** of the Paul Hamm debate, and support it with one **fact**.

____

____

Apply Your Knowledge **Think about the story "Save Every Sport!" and the articles you have read in this unit. Answer the questions below.**

Write the names of your favorite and least favorite sports. Then write two facts about each sport, followed by your overall opinion of the sport.

Favorite Sport: ______________________________

Fact: ______________________________

Fact: ______________________________

Opinion: ______________________________

____

Least Favorite Sport: ______________________________

Fact: ______________________________

Fact: ______________________________

Opinion: ______________________________

____

Choose a Team Project **Choose one of the following group activities, and complete it using your knowledge of sports.**

Sport Debate

With your group, choose a sport that some of you like and some don't. Then split into smaller groups that share the same opinion. In each smaller group, write a paragraph that uses facts to support why you do or do not like the chosen sport. Read the paragraphs on both sides to the class, and let them decide who wins the debate.

New Olympic Sport

In your group, think of a new team sport that combines parts of different existing sports. Write the rules of the new sport. Then make a list of reasons why this sport should be included in the Olympic Games. Include facts and opinions about the sport. Share your list with the class, and then ask their opinions about the new sport.

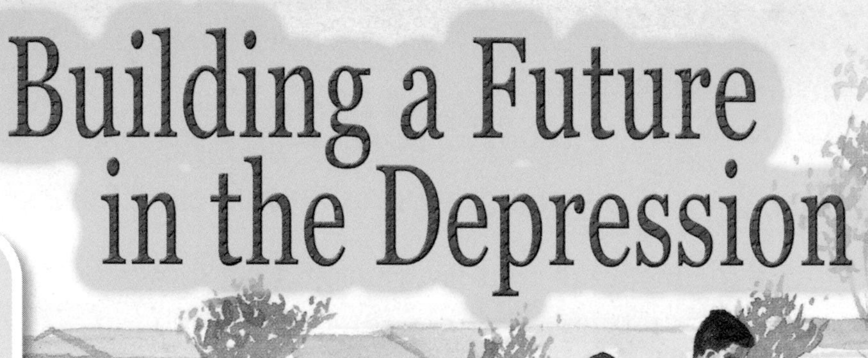

Building a Future in the Depression

Cause and Effect in Fiction

In a fiction story, events can **cause** other events to occur, which are called **effects.** Often, causes and effects happen one after another, creating a chain of effects.

- **Cause:** *During the Great Depression, many farms in Oklahoma and other states failed.*
- **Effect:** *As a result, a large number of people migrated to California to find work.*

Clue words such as *therefore, so, thus, as a result,* and *if... then* can help readers identify causes and effects.

Reader's Guide

Use the highlighted sentences and the Reader's Guide to identify causes and effects in this story.

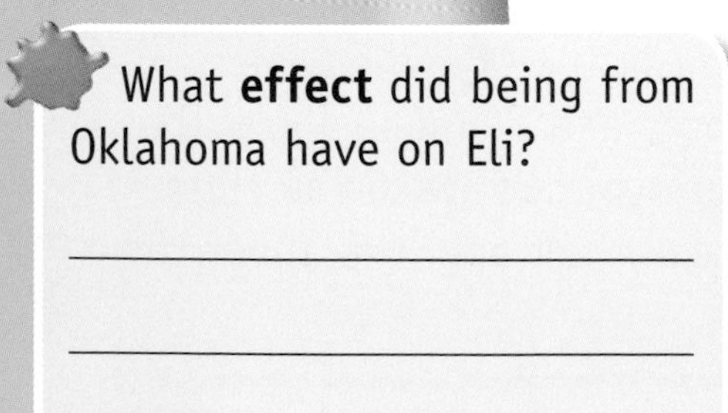

What **effect** did being from Oklahoma have on Eli?

____

____

____

"1939: More Americans Out of Work!" read the newspaper headline. Eli walked past the newspaper office in downtown Bakersfield, California, knowing well that there weren't any jobs for paperboys—even if there had been, he wouldn't have gotten one.

Eli was from Oklahoma, an "Okie," and it was nearly impossible for an Okie to get a job over someone from California. What Eli really wanted was to go to school, but Okies were not welcome in most local schools, so even school was off-limits to him. Eli worried that without an education, he would have no chance for a better future.

Eli's family had recently moved to California from the dusty fields outside Boise City, Oklahoma. Their farm had been ruined by terrible dust storms, and to make things even worse, the effects of the Great Depression had left a large number of workers jobless. The family had gone to California to find work on the farms there, but with very few jobs available, they spent most of their time in a government camp for farm workers.

One day, Eli was sitting in the camp outside of his family's tent when a truck drove up the road. A man stepped out of the truck, and Eli could tell from his new suit and necktie that the man was not from their camp.

Eli walked over to the man and said hello, trying to control his Oklahoma accent. He noticed that the man had a briefcase. "Can I help with your bag, sir?" Eli asked.

Mopping sweat off his forehead, the man looked down at Eli and smiled. "You can if you like, son, but what I really need is a tour. Would you mind showing me around?"

It turned out that the man's name was Mr. Hart, and he worked for the local school system. He was very interested in everything that was happening around Eli's camp, but especially in what was happening to the young people who weren't in school. When they finished the tour, Mr. Hart looked more thoughtful than ever.

"Is everything okay, sir?" Eli asked.

"With so many young people, what this camp needs is a school. I think we should build one," said Mr. Hart. Then he looked at Eli. "You strike me as a very helpful young man. If I convince the school system, will you help convince the others?"

What **caused** Eli's family to move to California?

1. ______________________________

____

2. ______________________________

____

Check Your Understanding

Do you:

__ look for causes and effects as you read?

__ predict what will happen next?

What **caused** Mr. Hart to think the camp needed a school?

____

____

____

Circle two clue words that show **causes** and **effects**.

Fill in the chart to show two **effects** of the **cause**.

Cause
The school opened.
Effects
1. ______________________
2. ______________________

"You can count on me, sir," said Eli.

Work on the school started right away. There was no money to hire workers, so Mr. Hart, the teachers, and the people who lived in the camp did all of the work themselves. Mr. Hart asked people in the community to donate what they didn't need and, therefore, was able to get free materials and supplies. Eli and the other young people of the camp helped Mr. Hart every step of the way.

Eli and his friends dug deep holes for the school's foundations. Blisters formed on their hands, and they worked on empty stomachs, but they kept working. Instead of going into town to look for jobs, young people and adults from the camp spent their mornings learning the basics of plumbing, carpentry, and stonework.

In 1940, the Arvin Federal Emergency School officially opened, so the camp families held a party to celebrate. Mr. Hart led the people of the camp on a tour of the buildings. For the first time in years, the families felt that a ray of hope had entered their difficult lives.

During the party, Eli excused himself and walked through the school again, feeling proud of his important work. As he did, he felt a tap on his shoulder. It was Mr. Hart. "I want to give you something, Eli, in recognition of all you have accomplished," he said. Then, feeling around inside the front pocket of his suit, Mr. Hart took out a shiny silver watch on a chain and handed it to Eli.

"This is so you always remember to make the most of the time you have," he said with a smile. "We built our own school, and you can build your own future."

Keep Thinking

Think about the story "Building a Future in the Depression." Circle the letter next to the best answer.

1. What **effect** did Eli think education would have on his life?
- **A** It would help him get a job as a paperboy.
- **B** His family could move back to Oklahoma.
- **C** He would be able to build a better future.
- **D** People would not call him "Okie" anymore.

2. What detail showed that Mr. Hart was not from the camp?
- **A** He worked for the school system.
- **B** He arrived at the camp in a truck.
- **C** He wore a new suit and necktie.
- **D** He wanted to build a school.

3. *During* the building of the school, Eli
- **A** gave Mr. Hart a tour of the camp.
- **B** read the daily newspaper.
- **C** was given a special pocket watch.
- **D** dug deep holes for the foundations.

Write your answers on the lines.

4. What **effect** did terrible dust storms have on Eli's family?

____

____

____

5. What **caused** Mr. Hart to think that Eli was a helpful young man?

____

____

6. Why do you think Eli left the party to walk through the school again?

____

____

____

Get Organized

Complete the chart below to show **causes** and **effects** in the story.

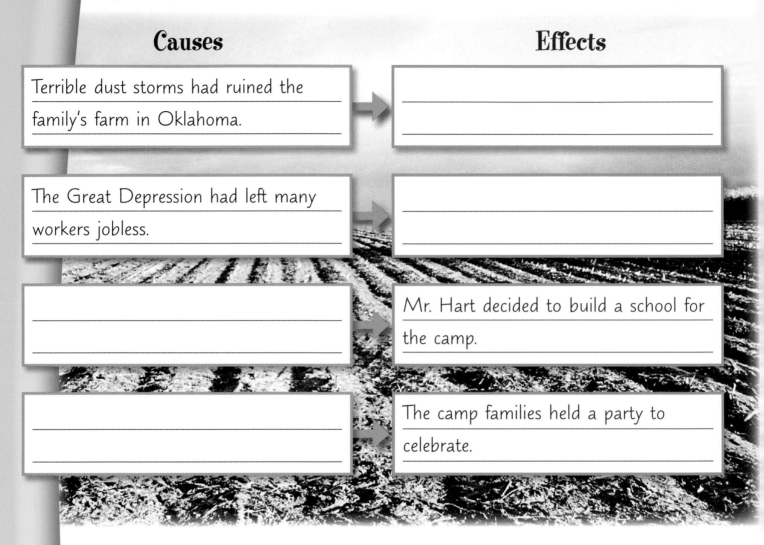

Causes	Effects
Terrible dust storms had ruined the family's farm in Oklahoma.	
The Great Depression had left many workers jobless.	
	Mr. Hart decided to build a school for the camp.
	The camp families held a party to celebrate.

Summarize

Imagine that you are Eli, and Mr. Hart has asked you to give a speech at the school's celebration party. Tell the way you came to the camp and why the school means so much to you.

Write Away!

Team Up

Work with a partner. Imagine two other ways that the students at the camp could have received an education before the camp school was built.

1. ______________________________

____

2. ______________________________

____

On Your Own

Suppose that you are a young person living in Eli's camp in 1939. Write a formal letter asking the school system to build a camp school. Explain why the young people of the camp need a school. Include **causes** and **effects.**

WRITER'S CHECKLIST

- ☐ Write a formal letter to the local school system.
- ☐ Explain your situation, including causes and effects.
- ☐ Persuade the school system that they should build a camp school.

LESSON 26

Cause and Effect in Science

In science articles, writers often show the way an event, or **cause**, can lead to another event, or **effect**. Sometimes many causes together can produce a single effect.

- **Cause 1:** *lack of rain*
- **Cause 2:** *heavy winds*
- **Cause 3:** *overgrazing*
- **Effect:** *the Dust Bowl*

Use the highlighted sentences and the Reader's Guide to identify causes and effects in this article.

During the years of the Great Depression, many American families were out of work. People struggled to survive. On April 13, 1935, in the middle of the Great Depression, American farmers were hit with another devastating blow. A whirlwind of dust turned the sky black above the southern plains. The dirt in the air was so thick that survivors of the day said they couldn't even see their hands in front of their faces.

The Dust Bowl occurred in the fourth year of an eight-year **drought** that lasted from 1931 to 1939. Five states in the region—Colorado, New Mexico, Kansas, Oklahoma, and Texas—were most affected. The terrible dust storms

Reader's Guide

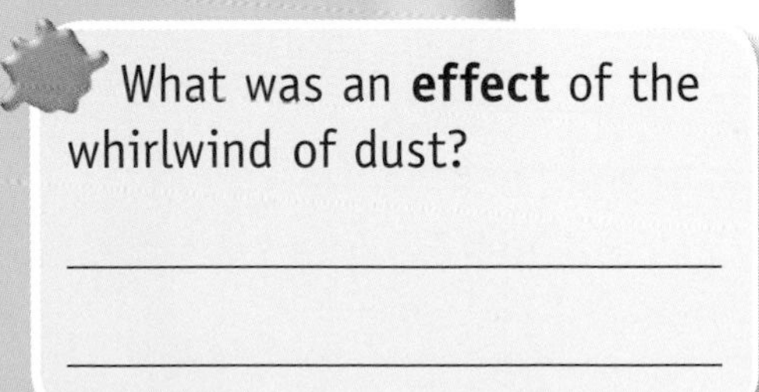

What was an **effect** of the whirlwind of dust?

____

____

drought a long period of dry weather

were caused by more than just a drought, however. Many causes collided to produce one of the worst decades for farmers in U.S. history.

Dust 'til Dawn

In the early 1900s, settlers were lured to the open grasslands of the southern plains by the promise of rich **topsoil** and plentiful harvests. The rain came frequently, and farmers reaped a good crop of wheat for many years.

When tractors appeared in the 1920s, many untouched grasslands were plowed to make room for more rows of wheat. Farmers prospered, and the land produced more crops than ever.

However, in the spring of 1931, the rain stopped. Many farmers believed the drought was temporary, so they continued to plow and plant their crops. Since they had only recently begun to farm the land in this region, they didn't know to expect long dry spells about once every 25 years. They watched in disbelief as the golden stems of wheat withered in the fields under the intense summer sun. Field after field was ruined.

▲ The long drought ruined many crops.

The soil of the southern plains became cracked and dry. Overgrazing by cattle and sheep on the remaining grasslands also stripped the soil of any remaining plants. By the time strong winds tore through the plains four years later, it was much too late to save the dry fields.

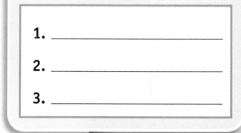

topsoil the fertile top layer of soil

What **caused** settlers to move to the southern plains in the early 1900s?

1. ______________________
2. ______________________
3. ______________________

Check Your Understanding

Do you:
_ look for effects with several causes?
_ picture descriptive details?

List three **causes** of the Dust Bowl.

1. ______________________
2. ______________________
3. ______________________

Gone with the Wind

erosion wearing away of soil

Without plant roots to hold the soil in place, the fierce winds caused massive **erosion**. Strong gusts of wind blew the dry topsoil right off the fields. Like gigantic ocean waves, a great mass of dust swept across the flat open land. Mounds of soil collected like tall snowdrifts against fences and buildings.

Wind-blown dust piled high against buildings.

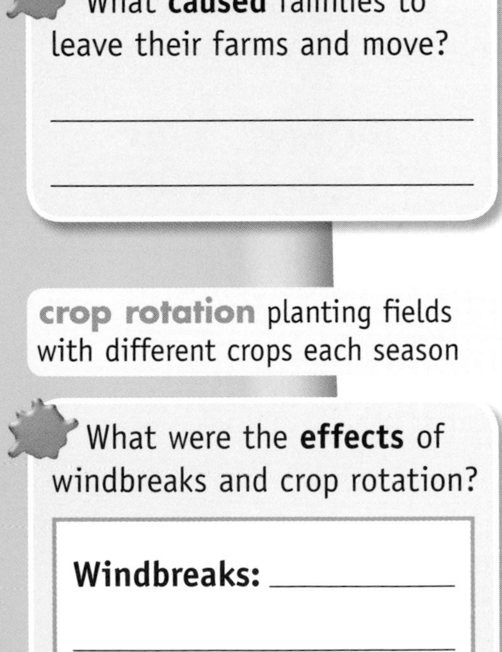

What **caused** families to leave their farms and move?

____

____

crop rotation planting fields with different crops each season

What were the **effects** of windbreaks and crop rotation?

Windbreaks: ____________

____

____

Crop rotation: ____________

____

____

After many years without crops to sell, thousands of families were forced to abandon their farms and move west to California. There, they hoped to find jobs on farms that had not been affected by the drought. There were far too many workers for the few available jobs, however. Many families were forced to live in tents or tiny shacks without plumbing or electricity.

Singing in the Rain

In 1935, at the height of the drought, the U.S. government passed some laws to improve farming practices. Trees were planted along the edges of fields. These rows of trees, called windbreaks, helped stop big gusts of wind from reaching crops. **Crop rotation** kept soil healthy and prevented erosion. These practices are still in use today.

The rain finally fell again in 1939. Survivors remember dancing excitedly in the rain. It took time, but farms in the southern plains began to prosper once again.

Even though the Dust Bowl occurred more than 75 years ago, its effects are still being felt today. We can't prevent another drought, but responsible farming methods can help prevent a devastating dust storm from occurring again.

Keep Thinking

Think about the article "Blown Away: The Dust Bowl." Circle the letter next to the best answer.

1. What was one **effect** of the 1931–1939 drought?
- **A** Farmers moved to the southern plains.
- **B** Crops died, and fields were ruined.
- **C** Farmers kept plowing and planting crops.
- **D** Tractors appeared in the 1920s.

2. What happened *first* in the events leading up to the Dust Bowl?
- **A** A long drought and overgrazing stripped the soil of plants.
- **B** Fierce winds turned the sky black with dust.
- **C** Farmers abandoned their land and moved west.
- **D** Mounds of soil collected like snowdrifts.

3. What is the main idea of the article?
- **A** The Great Depression was a hard time for American families.
- **B** Farming practices caused a drought that led to the Dust Bowl.
- **C** Settlers never should have moved to the southern plains.
- **D** The Dust Bowl was the result of many different causes.

Write your answers on the lines.

4. Write a sentence that explains the **effect** of tractors on farming in the 1920s.

____

____

5. Why did the drought come as a surprise to many farmers in the southern plains?

____

____

____

6. What **effects** of the Dust Bowl might farmers still experience today?

____

____

____

Get Organized

Fill in the diagram to show **causes and effects** during the Dust Bowl.

Cause	+	Cause	=	Effect
The southern plains had rich topsoil.	+	The rain came frequently.	=	
	+		=	Wheat withered in the fields.
	+		=	Fierce winds blew the dry topsoil off the fields.

Summarize

Imagine that you were a settler on the southern plains during the Dust Bowl. Historians have asked you to describe what it was like to have lived through it. Write a paragraph that describes what you saw and how you felt.

Write Away!

Team Up

Work with a partner. Imagine that you can travel back in time to 1920. What three changes would you make that might change the outcome of the Dust Bowl?

1. ______________________________

2. ______________________________

3. ______________________________

On Your Own

Suppose that the year is 1920, and you have traveled back in time to speak to a group of farmers. Write a speech that explains the **causes** and **effects** of the Dust Bowl. Describe a few ways that farmers can prevent it from happening.

WRITER'S CHECKLIST

- ☐ Write a speech to give to farmers in 1920.
- ☐ Explain the causes and effects of the Dust Bowl.
- ☐ Tell farmers how they can prevent the Dust Bowl from happening.

LESSON 27

Battling the GREAT DEPRESSION

Cause and Effect in Social Studies

A **cause** is the reason something happens, and an **effect** is what happens as a result.

- **Cause:** *During the Great Depression, banks ran out of money.*
- **Effect:** *People lost their life savings.*

Social studies articles often describe a chain of causes and effects that happened over a period of time.

Reader's Guide

What were two **effects** of the Great Depression?

1. ______________________

____

2. ______________________

____

Use the highlighted sentences and the Reader's Guide to identify causes and effects in this article.

When historians list the hardest times the United States has ever faced, one stands out above the rest: the depression of the 1930s, known as the Great Depression. During this time, businesses failed by the thousands, putting 15 million people—nearly one fourth of the labor force—out of work. Hunger and poverty reached every corner of the United States. Never before or since had Americans known such economic disaster.

Heading for a Crash

In the early 1920s, many Americans bought things on credit. Working people used credit to buy exciting—and expensive—new items such as refrigerators, washing machines, cars, and houses. It appeared that people had a lot of money. Actually, they were deep in debt.

At the same time, many **investors** were also borrowing money to buy stocks. When stock prices rose, they would sell the stocks at a profit. Instead of paying off loans, they would use the money to buy more stocks. These "paper millionaires" owned millions of dollars worth of stock, but went millions of dollars into debt to purchase it. They could only make money if the stock market kept rising.

investors people who buy and sell stock in companies

And rise it did, until October 1929, when stock prices began to fall. Nervous investors began selling stock before the prices got too low, which only drove stock prices lower. Investors began to panic, and on October 24, 1929, more than 16 million shares of stock were sold. The stock market had crashed.

What **caused** the stock market to crash?

____

____

____

The Snowball Effect

The crash of the stock market quickly spread chaos to every aspect of life in the United States. First, it brought down the banks. Banks were unable to collect on the huge loans they had made to investors, businesses, and working Americans. Thousands of banks were forced to close. As a result, many people lost their life savings.

Businesses also lost money when the banks failed. As a result, many businesses had to shut down or lay off most of their employees. Unemployment soared, which started a vicious circle: unemployed people couldn't afford to buy much, so businesses cut back on how much they produced. This led to layoffs and business closings, which caused even more unemployment.

List three **effects** of the stock market crash.

1. ________________________

2. ________________________

3. ________________________

Long lines of unemployed people gathered anywhere food was given away.

Check Your Understanding

Do you:

__ ask what caused events to happen?

__ look for a chain of causes and effects?

bankrupt unable to pay off debt

Put a ✓ next to each way neighbors helped each other.

	shared what they had
	ended the Great Depression
	gathered to sing and read aloud
	held "rent parties"

What was an **effect** of the Great Depression on society?

___

___

___

Facing Hardship Together

Most Americans faced an economic nightmare. Many were unable to pay off their debts and went **bankrupt**, losing their homes and possessions. Even families without any debt used up what little money they had to pay rent until they found work, only to lose their homes when no work appeared. People with no money to buy food had to stand in line for hours, only to receive a small bag of flour and some dried peas with which to feed their families.

Americans turned to each other for help. Neighbors shared what they had and gathered to sing songs and read books aloud when there was no money to go to the movies or buy a radio. They held "rent parties," where each guest brought a little money to help the most struggling families.

Recovery Begins

When President Franklin D. Roosevelt took office in 1933, he told Americans, "The only thing we have to fear is fear itself." His plan, the New Deal, provided aid to the poor and insured the money in banks. It also created government programs such as the Works Progress Administration (WPA) to give people jobs. Americans responded to Roosevelt's hopefulness and began to put the money they earned back into banks. Slowly, the economy improved.

▲ Government programs like the WPA put people back to work.

The Great Depression was the worst economic disaster in U.S. history, and its effects on society were enormous. When the hard times were over, people felt a sense of pride in having made it through. Battling the Great Depression gave people confidence that Americans could overcome hardships if they worked together.

Keep Thinking

Think about the article "Battling the Great Depression." Circle the letter next to the best answer.

1. Why did people need to keep working in order to keep their belongings?
- **A** because they had bought many stocks
- **B** because they had used credit to buy them
- **C** because the banks had failed
- **D** because the stock market had crashed

2. In the 1920s, how were investors and ordinary people alike?
- **A** Both bought stocks on credit.
- **B** Both made millions on the stock market.
- **C** Both were bankrupt.
- **D** Both went into debt to buy things.

3. How do you think "paper millionaires" got their name?
- **A** They printed their own money on paper.
- **B** They were too poor to buy paper.
- **C** They were only millionaires on paper.
- **D** They owned millions of dollars worth of paper.

Write your answers on the lines.

4. List two **effects** that resulted from the failure of banks.

____

____

____

5. What **caused** people to start putting money back into banks?

____

____

____

6. Why did many people lose their homes during the Depression?

____

____

Get Organized

Fill in the flow chart to show **causes** and **effects** during the Great Depression.

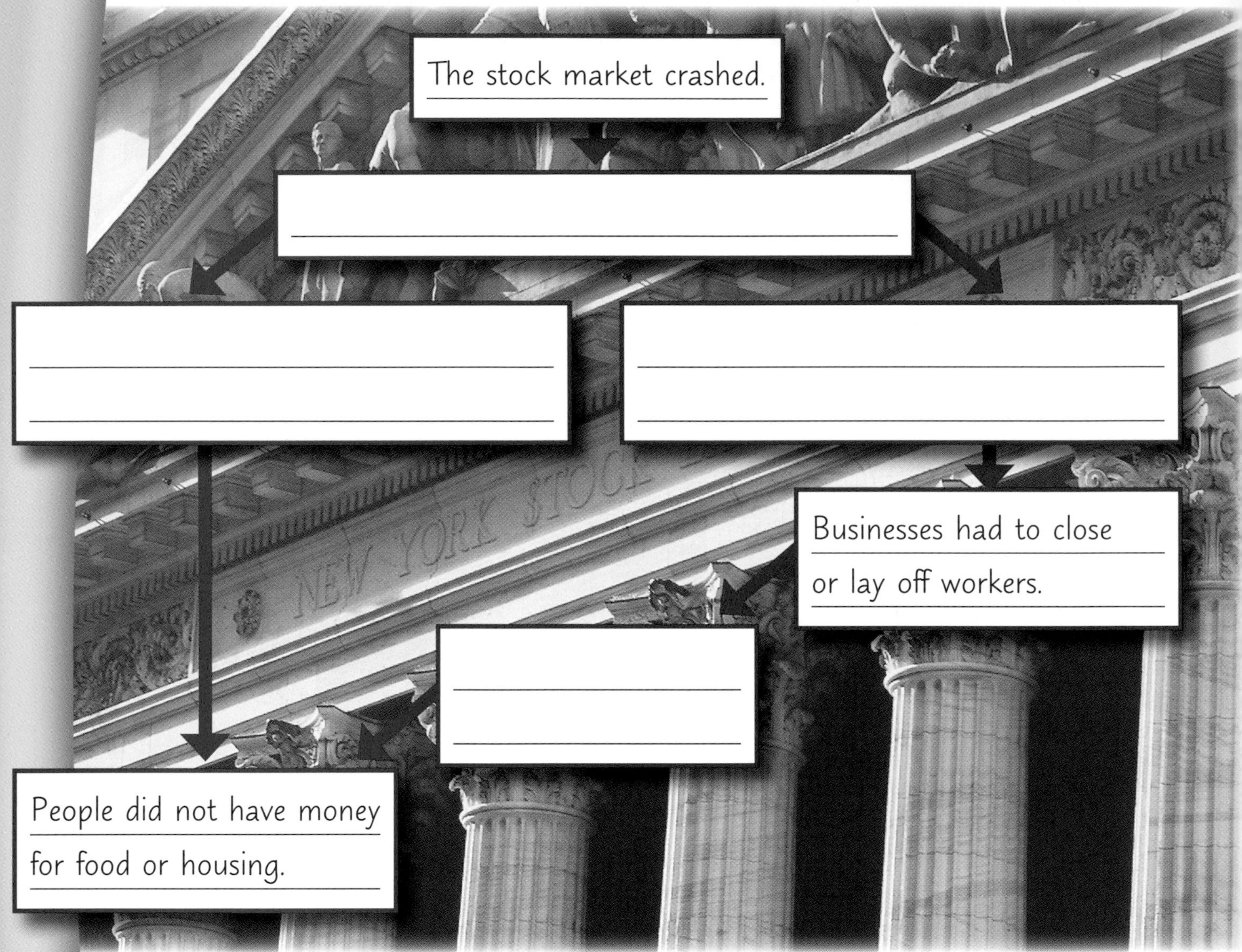
The stock market crashed.
Businesses had to close or lay off workers.
People did not have money for food or housing.
NEW YORK STOCK

Summarize

Imagine that you are keeping a journal during the Great Depression. Write a short entry that describes what might happen if an adult in your family lost his or her job.

Write Away!

Team Up

Suppose that you are an investor in the stock market in 1929. Stock prices have started to fall, and you must decide what to do. With a partner, discuss each of the following choices, and then list their possible effects below.

You panic and sell all of your stock. ______________________________

____

You stay calm and keep your stock. ______________________________

____

On Your Own

Write a short story about a stock investor who helps prevent the Great Depression. Write about the choices he or she made and the effects they had on history.

WRITER'S CHECKLIST

- ☐ Write a short story set in 1929.
- ☐ Explain the investor's choices and why he or she made them.
- ☐ Describe the effects of the investor's decisions.

Unemployment Rates

Cause and Effect in Math

In math, numbers can represent **causes** and **effects.** Learning about causes and effects can help readers understand the effects that events such as the Great Depression had on people's lives.

- **Cause:** *On October 29, 1929, the stock market crashed.*
- **Effects:** *Five thousand banks failed. Thirty-two thousand businesses went bankrupt. Unemployment soared.*

Gather Information **Before the stock market crash in 1929, the percentage of unemployed workers was 3%. Afterwards, the unemployment rate rose dramatically. Study the chart below to see the unemployment rate each year from 1929 to 1940.**

Annual Unemployment Rate

Year	Percent Unemployed	Year	Percent Unemployed
1929	3%	**1935**	20%
1930	9%	**1936**	17%
1931	16%	**1937**	14%
1932	24%	**1938**	19%
1933	25%	**1939**	17%
1934	22%	**1940**	15%

Understand a Line Graph

A line graph can help readers see the way unemployment changed over time. Study the graph below. Then use the graph and the chart to answer the questions.

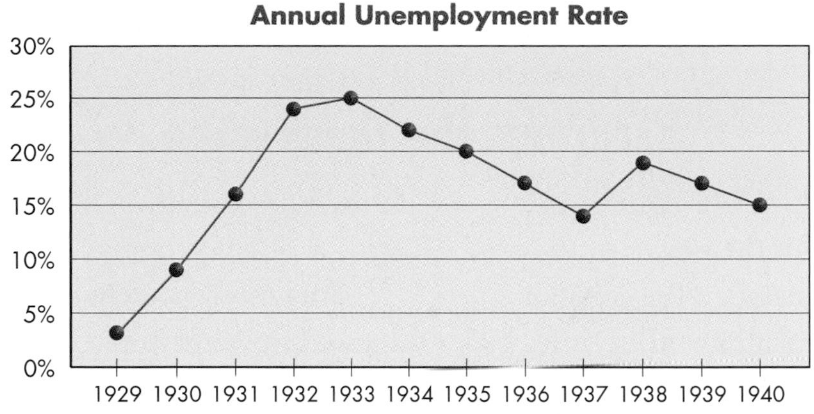

1. In which year was unemployment the highest?

____

2. Was the unemployment rate higher or lower in 1940 than it was in 1929?

____

3. Do you think the **effects** of the Great Depression lasted past 1940? Explain.

____

____

Make Your Own Line Graph

The chart below shows the average income for working families from 1929–1933. Use the chart to complete the line graph. Tell a possible cause of the changes in income.

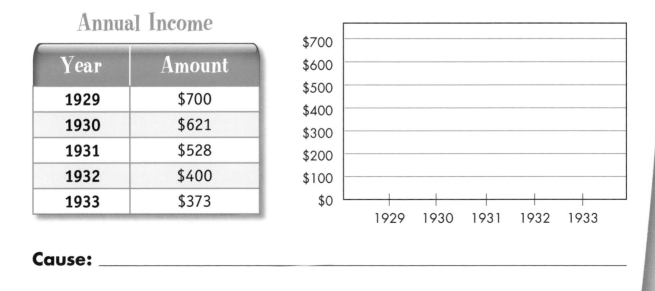

Annual Income

Year	Amount
1929	$700
1930	$621
1931	$528
1932	$400
1933	$373

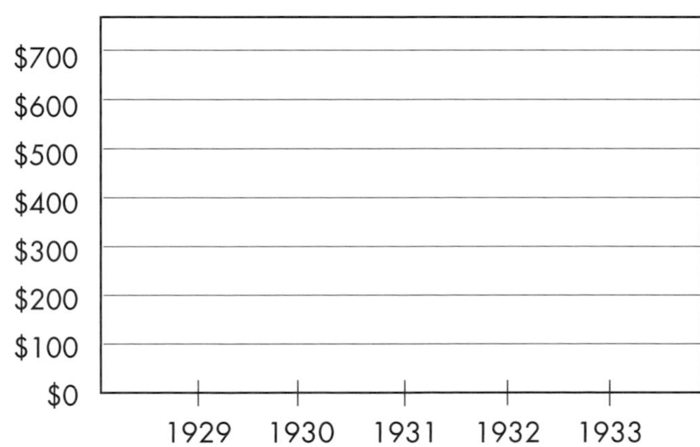

Cause: ____

____

Making Connections

Read the article below. Then answer the questions.

Escaping the Depression

During 1935, U.S. President Franklin D. Roosevelt said this about the power of movies: "During the Depression, when the spirit of the people is lower than at any other time, it is a splendid thing that for just 15 cents an American can go to a movie and look at the smiling face of a baby and forget his troubles."

In the early 1930s, the United States was suffering through the worst economic disaster in its history. Even with hardship affecting their daily lives, 60–70 million Americans—about half the U.S. population—filled movie theaters each week! What caused so many people to spend their hard-earned money on movies?

Hollywood film studios wanted to keep audiences in movie theaters. They tried to make movies that would help people forget about their troubles for a little while. They made many gangster films, musicals, family films, and comedies. Many of these movies told stories of progress and hope.

Some movies during the Great Depression showed the hardships of life at the time. The movie *Gold Diggers* was a musical about a millionaire who created a Broadway show just so unemployed actors could have work. Other movies, such as *The Wizard of Oz*, told stories of fantasy worlds that audiences were able to escape into.

Most movies showed hard times, but gave a positive twist at the end. People going to the movies in the Great Depression had something fun to look forward to, and that made it worth their 15 cents.

1. What was one **effect** of going to the movies during the Great Depression?

____

2. What does the writer think **caused** people to spend money on movies?

____

3. What do you think **caused** many movies during the Great Depression to tell stories of progress and hope?

____

____

Apply Your Knowledge **Think about the story "Building a Future in the Depression" and the articles you have read in this unit. Answer the questions below.**

In your opinion, what would have been the hardest part of living during the Great Depression?

____

____

____

____

____

Describe what you would have done to help your family survive the economic disaster.

____

____

____

____

____

Choose a Team Project **Choose one of the following group activities, and complete it using your knowledge of the Great Depression.**

Make a Financial Plan

What would you do if the stock market crashed tomorrow? In your group, discuss ways that your families could work together to survive a depression. List suggestions for each family, and then combine them into a single financial plan. Read the plan to the class, and talk about its possible effects.

Be a Filmmaker

With your group, talk about the kinds of movies audiences wanted to see during the Great Depression. Then think of a new idea for a movie that might have been successful during the 1930s. Write a description of the movie, and draw a movie poster. Share your poster and description with the class.

LESSON 29

Mystery on the 13th Floor

Problems and Solutions in Fiction

In many fiction stories, a character or group of characters needs to find the **solution** to a **problem**.

- **Problem:** *Zach, Tiffany, and Yolanda wondered what they were going to do all Saturday.*
- **Solution:** *The police asked them to help solve a mystery.*

Writers often include story clues that help readers predict the solution to a problem.

Reader's Guide

Use the highlighted sentences and the Reader's Guide to identify problems and solutions in this story.

One Saturday morning, Zach, Yolanda, and Tiffany were sitting in a local diner wondering what they were going to do all day. Then they got a call, and it wasn't just any call. It was the police. Yolanda's father, Detective Perez, was downtown, phoning from the Regal Hotel, where the 10th annual World Archaeology Convention was being held. A priceless artifact had been stolen, and Detective Perez knew the Enigmas would want to check it out.

The teens were known as the Enigmas because they had an amazing talent for solving mysteries. Zach had a knack for chemistry, and Yolanda was good at figuring out logic puzzles. When Tiffany wasn't solving mysteries, she spent her time in drama club working on various disguises.

Predict a way Tiffany might help **solve** the mystery.

____

____

When they reached the hotel, Detective Perez pulled them aside. "Someone stole the Statue of Light, an ancient African treasure, from the ballroom on the 13th floor," he said. "Come with me, and I'll show you." He led them to the service elevator, where they had to squeeze in beside a housekeeper with a large cleaning cart. At the 13th floor, the elevator opened up into the huge grand ballroom.

Detective Perez pointed out the empty pedestal where the statue had been. "Our investigators have already collected the evidence they need to run their tests, so you can go ahead and take a look before housekeeping cleans things up." Taking out their rubber gloves and forensics kits, the Enigmas got to work.

Right away, Zach saw a spot on the floor that was lighter than the dark blue color of the carpet. Looking closer, he saw that there was powder between the carpet's fibers. Zach gathered some of the powder and tested it with a solution in his chemistry kit. He quickly identified it as powdered bathroom cleaner. This was strange because the housekeeping staff had not yet cleaned the 13th floor.

Next, Tiffany discovered a long, blonde hair that had fallen near the statue's display stand. She picked it up with tweezers and placed it in a clean evidence bag.

Yolanda stood nearby holding her camera and thought about the clues—something just didn't make sense. The statue was big, and people would have noticed the thief carrying it, but no one had. She looked down and noticed how easily her feet left prints in the thick carpet, and then she noticed a pair of strange lines in the carpet near the doorway. The lines looked like they could have been left by wheels.

What was the **problem** in the highlighted sentences?

____

____

What skills did Zach use to find out what made the spot on the floor?

____

____

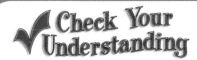

Check Your Understanding

Do you:

__ find story problems?

__ look for clues to predict the solutions?

What clues helped Detective Perez find the **solution** below?

Clue 1: ____________________

____

Clue 2: ____________________

____

Solution: One housekeeper had blonde hair, but was wearing a disguise.

Name three things the Frog Burglar did to steal the statue without getting caught.

1. ____________________

____

2. ____________________

____

3. ____________________

____

Yolanda wondered where she had seen wheels like that before, and suddenly she knew—the cleaning cart in the elevator. Someone had been in the room with a cart of cleaning supplies, and that person had used the cart to get the statue out secretly!

The group gathered their evidence and hurried down to the basement of the hotel, where Detective Perez asked the manager to call the housekeeping staff together. As soon as everyone was there, the Enigmas realized they had a problem: none of the housekeepers were blonde. Tiffany softly whispered something to Detective Perez.

"I'll handle this," Detective Perez said, walking up to the staff. He stopped beside a woman with freckles and bright red hair. He looked at her closely and then said, "How long have you worn a red wig?" The woman's face went pale. The detective then pulled a long, blonde hair from her shoulder and said, "There aren't many redheads with blonde hair on their clothes." While the other officers searched the woman's housekeeping cart, Detective Perez led her off for questioning.

The police soon discovered that the housekeeper was the famous Frog Burglar, an art thief and master of disguise who hopped from one city to another to keep a step ahead of police. She had joined the hotel staff just to have access to the priceless statue.

The police were grateful to the Enigmas for solving an important case and invited the teens to become special youth members of their forensics team. When Detective Perez insisted that it would only be on weekends, the Enigmas quickly realized that it would be a long time before they had to face another boring Saturday.

Keep Thinking

Think about the story "Mystery on the 13th Floor." Circle the letter next to the best answer.

1. What did the clue Tiffany found suggest about the thief who stole the statue?
   - **A** The thief probably wore a wig.
   - **B** The thief probably had long, blonde hair.
   - **C** The thief was probably a housekeeper.
   - **D** The thief was probably the Frog Burglar.

2. What caused Yolanda to realize that the statue had been hidden in a cleaning cart?
   - **A** She saw wheel marks and remembered the cart she had seen.
   - **B** There was a blonde hair on the floor behind the statue stand.
   - **C** She stood nearby with her camera and took pictures.
   - **D** She knew there was a new housekeeper on the hotel's staff.

3. What can you infer that Tiffany whispered to Detective Perez?
   - **A** She told him to call the housekeeping staff together.
   - **B** She told him that none of the housekeepers were blonde.
   - **C** She told him about the red-haired housekeeper's disguise.
   - **D** She told him that the Frog Burglar would soon strike again.

Write your answers on the lines.

4. What **problem** did joining the police forensics team **solve** for the Enigmas?

___

___

5. Why was it NOT a **problem** for the Enigmas to examine the crime scene?

___

___

___

6. How did Zach determine what made the spot on the floor?

___

___

___

Get Organized

Fill in the boxes below to show different **problems** and **solutions** in the story.

Frog Burglar

Problem

She needed to get close enough to steal the statue.

Solution

______

Problem

She needed to keep one step ahead of the police.

Solution

______

The Enigmas

Problem

No one had seen the statue leave the ballroom.

Solution

______

Problem

None of the hotel housekeepers were blonde.

Solution

______

Summarize

The magazine *Forensics Today* is running an article about the events at the Regal Hotel. What might it say about the mystery and those who solved it?

______

Write Away!

Team Up

With a partner, imagine two other clues the Enigmas might have found at the scene of the crime. Explain the way each clue could have helped them **solve** the mystery.

Clue 1: ______________________________

____

Clue 2: ______________________________

____

On Your Own

Write the back cover of a new mystery book about the Enigmas. Include story elements, such as characters, setting, and the **problem** the group must **solve.**

WRITER'S CHECKLIST

- ☐ Write a summary of a new mystery story about the Enigmas.
- ☐ Include the important story elements.
- ☐ Describe the problem that the characters must solve.

LESSON 30

Forensics: Crime Scene Science

Problems and Solutions in Science

Scientists must identify **problems** and try to find possible **solutions**. Science articles often describe the way scientists solve specific problems. One solution may solve more than one problem.

- **Problem 1:** *Police need to trace stolen goods.*
- **Problem 2:** *Investigators need clues to search for a missing person.*
- **Solution:** *Forensic science can help solve different kinds of mysteries.*

Reader's Guide

forensic scientists experts who use science to solve crimes

Name three **problems** that forensic scientists can help **solve**.

1. ______________________
2. ______________________
3. ______________________

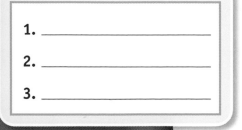

Use the highlighted sentences and the Reader's Guide to find problems and solutions in this article.

Police investigators are on the scene at a jewelry store robbery. Even without witnesses, the **forensic scientists** are confident that they will solve the crime. They have found blood on a broken window and fingerprints and footprints inside the store. One officer found tiny blue fibers and a hair. Outside, there were fresh tire tracks.

Police depend on evidence like this to solve crimes. Every crime scene has its own unique set of clues. Forensic scientists collect the evidence and study it with scientific tools to solve many different kinds of mysteries, including robberies, missing persons, and murders. Some evidence, such as fingerprints, can be linked to a specific person.

However, most evidence is not unique. Scientists need to consider many pieces of evidence to solve a crime.

Finger Tips

Since every fingerprint is unique, fingerprints can provide strong evidence that points to a specific person. At a crime scene, fingerprints are dusted with a special chemical, photographed, and, if possible, lifted. Later, a fingerprint expert scans the prints into a computer.

Prints from the crime scene are then compared to prints from possible suspects by examining tiny details, such as loops, swirls, and ridges. The expert also compares the crime scene prints to fingerprints in a national database. An exact match shows that a specific person was at the scene of the crime.

How can fingerprints help **solve** the **problem** of linking a suspect to a crime?

____

____

Blood Work

Blood found at a crime scene can be analyzed in different ways. Human blood contains substances that are used to classify blood into four main **blood types**: A, B, AB, and O. Blood type information can help narrow down a list of suspects, but it can't point to a specific person. Many people have the same blood type.

The **DNA** in blood can provide a more specific match. DNA is a substance found in living cells that is unique for each person. DNA is found in blood as well as other cells in the human body, including skin, saliva, and hair roots.

The DNA code looks like a pattern of dark and light bands. Scientists compare the DNA code from blood found at the crime scene to the DNA code from a sample from a suspect. If the pattern of bands from both samples is the same, the scientist has strong evidence that the blood from the crime scene came from the suspect.

blood types categories of human blood based on chemistry

What is the **problem** with using blood types?

____

____

____

DNA a code found in living cells

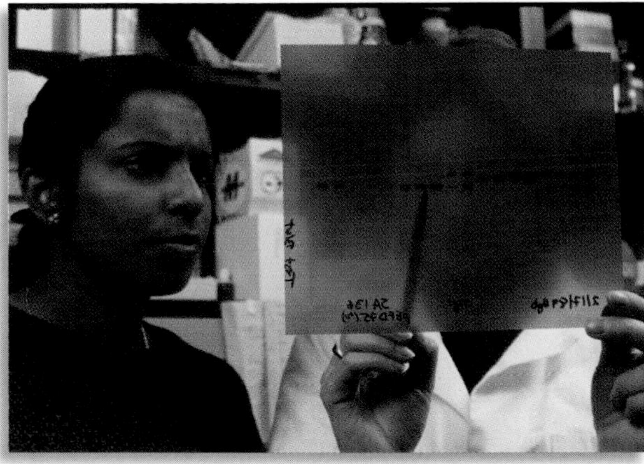

◀ Forensic scientists compare DNA codes to match evidence to a suspect.

Check Your Understanding

Do you:

__ look for problems as you read?

__ predict the possible solutions?

What can be a **problem** in using shoe or tire evidence?

____

____

trace evidence tiny pieces of material left at a crime scene

Fill in the chart with the **problem** and **solution** from the highlighted sentences.

Problem
____
____

Solution
____
____
____

Making Tracks

Shoe prints or tire tracks found at a crime scene can also be valuable evidence. Shoe and tire treads come in many patterns, but they are not unique. They can hold clues that may help identify a suspect, however.

Investigators use the size and pattern of a tire tread to help pinpoint the type of car or shoe that made the track. Some parts of a shoe or tire tread may develop unique wear patterns. These small differences in wear can help link an individual to the scene of a crime.

Tiny Traces

Even the smallest pieces of evidence can help solve a crime. It can be hard to find tiny clues such as bits of soil, paint chips, glass, hairs, or clothing fibers. Experts collect this **trace evidence** by going over a crime scene inch by inch. Experts examine trace evidence with a microscope and then compare it to similar materials found with a suspect. Most trace evidence is not unique, but it can help narrow down a list of suspects.

In studying fibers, experts look at color, length, and thickness. Fibers are not unique—a blue fiber could come from any brand of blue jeans. However, fibers that are proven to be very similar can suggest a link between a suspect and a crime.

Many different kinds of evidence are found at a crime scene. Using scientific tools, forensic scientists analyze the evidence and use it to link suspects to the scene of the crime. The information forensic scientists uncover can solve many different mysteries.

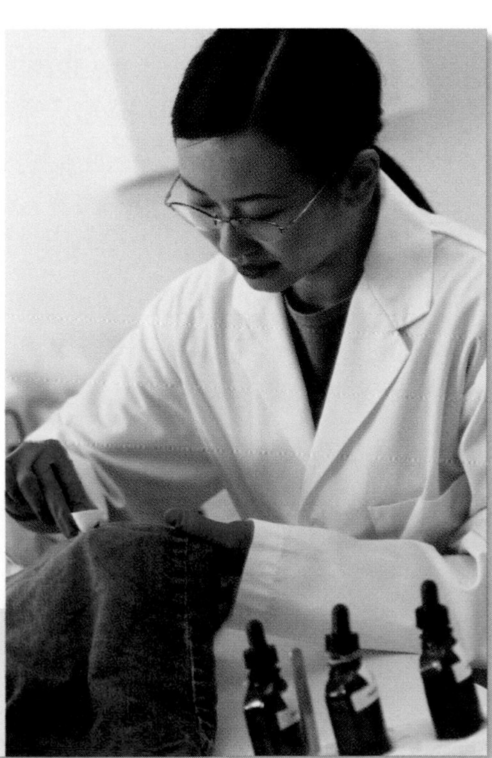

▶ Forensic scientists carefully examine all the evidence.

Keep Thinking

Think about the article "Forensics: Crime Scene Science." Circle the letter next to the best answer.

1. What is a **problem** with using shoe and tire treads to identify a suspect?
A They are not unique.
B They are hard to see.
C They have nothing to do with who committed the crime.
D Some parts of the tread may be more worn than others.

2. What is the main idea of the article?
A Forensic scientists can only solve a crime if they have good evidence.
B Forensic scientists use different kinds of evidence to solve crimes.
C The smallest pieces of evidence are always the biggest clues.
D Tire treads can help lead investigators to a suspect.

3. Which sentence best compares fingerprint evidence and DNA evidence?
A Fingerprints are unique, but DNA is the same for everyone.
B Fingerprints can narrow down the field of suspects, but DNA cannot.
C Fingerprints and DNA can both identify a specific person.
D Fingerprints and DNA are both examined by studying tiny loops and swirls.

Write your answers on the lines.

4. How can tire tracks help investigators **solve** the **problem** of finding a suspect?

____

____

5. The size of trace evidence can be a **problem**. How do forensic scientists **solve** it?

____

____

____

6. What **problem** do you think is created when criminals wear gloves?

____

____

____

Get Organized

Fill in the chart to show possible **problems** and **solutions** a forensic scientist might face.

Problems	Solutions
The fingerprints at the crime scene don't match any of the suspects.	
The blood found has a very common blood type.	
Shoe prints were found, but they don't have any unique features.	
None of the trace evidence was unique to a specific person.	

Summarize

Imagine that you are a newspaper reporter writing a feature on a team of forensic scientists where you live. Write the first paragraph of an article summarizing what they do.

Write Away!

Team Up

Work with a partner. Imagine that you are a pair of detectives working to **solve** a case of stolen computers. Think of three specific pieces of evidence that you might find at the crime scene. List your ideas below.

1. ______________________________

2. ______________________________

3. ______________________________

On Your Own

Imagine that you are using forensic science to **solve** the case above. Write a report analyzing the three pieces of evidence you listed and using them to solve the crime.

WRITER'S CHECKLIST

- ☐ Describe the evidence.
- ☐ Explain the way you would analyze each piece of evidence.
- ☐ Use the evidence to draw conclusions about one or more suspects.

LESSON 31

Everyone Leaves a Mark

Problems and Solutions in Social Studies

Social studies articles often present information about social **problems**. Some of these problems have several possible **solutions**. Readers can determine which solution best solves the problem.

- **Problem:** *It is sometimes difficult to identify people accurately.*
- **Solution 1:** *Give people an identifying mark.*
- **Solution 2:** *Check their fingerprints.*

Reader's Guide

What **problem** do fingerprints help **solve**?

____

____

Use the highlighted sentences and the Reader's Guide to identify problems and solutions in this article.

No matter how similar two people may appear to be, one thing is distinctive—their fingerprints. It is now common knowledge that fingerprints are unique, but this was not always believed. In fact, fingerprints have only been widely used to identify people for about 100 years.

Classifying Fingerprints

Fingerprints are classified in three main ways: by the patterns made by their curves and shapes, by where the patterns are positioned on the finger, and by their overall size, which is determined by counting and tracing the ridges in them.

No two fingerprints are identical. In fact, even the fingerprints of identical twins are unique. Every finger has a unique ridge pattern that does not change with age.

This feature makes fingerprints a reliable means of personal identification. Forensic scientists rely on this powerful tool to distinguish one person from another. This development has greatly helped law enforcement.

Fingerprints can be used to **verify** a person's identity or to determine whether a suspect has been at a crime scene. Computer programs allow millions of prints to be quickly identified. Even partial prints can be used to identify suspects. However, it took years to convince people that fingerprints could identify people reliably.

Why is fingerprinting a **solution** to the **problem** of identifying people?

1. ______________________

____

2. ______________________

____

verify to make sure that something is true

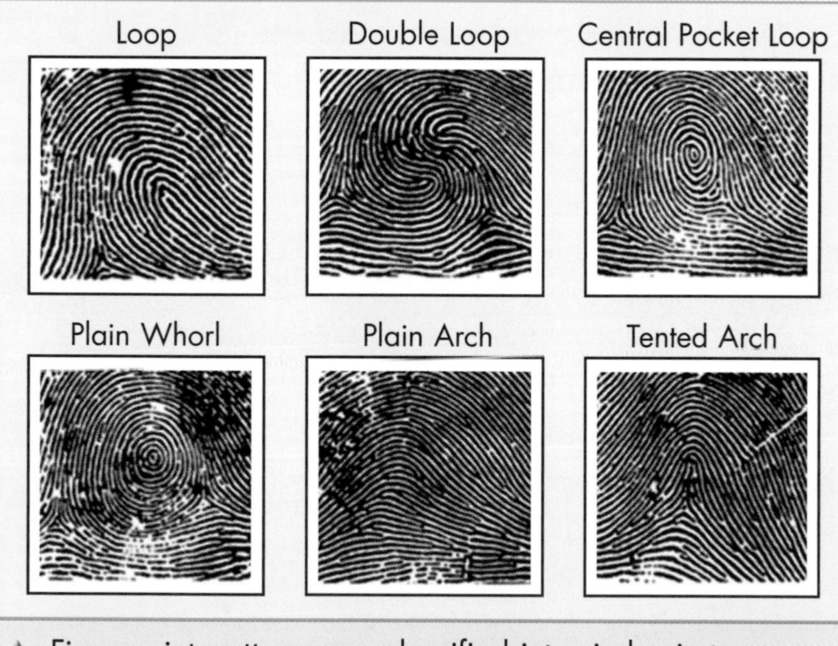

▲ Fingerprint patterns are classified into six basic types.

Check Your Understanding

Do you:

__ look for solutions to problems as you read?

__ ask if one solution might be better than another?

Before Fingerprinting

Before the wide use of fingerprints, people used other ways to identify people. In earlier civilizations, criminals were marked so that they could be identified later. The Romans tattooed their soldiers for the same reasons. In more recent times, police relied on witnesses to identify suspects by sight. However, memory is not perfect, and people can easily change their physical appearances.

In the 1870s, a French scientist tried to establish an identification system based on bone measurements. He believed that bone measurements would be a unique and consistent way to identify a person.

What are two **problems** with relying on witnesses to identify suspects?

1. ______________________

____

2. ______________________

____

What showed that fingerprinting was a better **solution** than using bone measurements?

____

____

____

____

latent present but not yet visible

The system was used for nearly 30 years until two men were discovered who had exactly the same bone measurements. Although they looked strikingly similar and had identical measurements, they were clearly two separate people. Fingerprinting the two men showed that even though they were similar in many ways, their fingerprints were distinctly different.

History of Fingerprinting

Fingerprints were not widely used for personal identification until the late 1800s, when **latent** fingerprints were discovered. Around that time, scientists found that any contact between a fingertip and a surface would create a latent print. Dusting a surface with a fine powder and chemicals could reveal the fingerprints that had previously been invisible. This development was the beginning of "the age of scientific crime detection."

▲ Fingerprints can be revealed by dusting them with a fine powder and chemicals.

How could having millions of fingerprints on file help **solve** a **problem**?

____

____

____

Law enforcement officers began to use fingerprinting techniques to solve crimes of all kinds. By the end of the 1930s, millions of fingerprints were on file. The first case in which a person was convicted of a crime based solely on fingerprint evidence happened in 1937.

The use of fingerprints to identify crime suspects was a tremendous step forward for law enforcement. Today, the field of forensic science is booming, thanks in part to the success of fingerprinting. Thousands of people work in forensic science careers in crime labs all over the world. Forensic science owes much of this growth to the science of fingerprinting. Forensic scientists still rely on these unique marks to identify people and solve crimes.

Keep Thinking

Think about the article "Everyone Leaves a Mark." Circle the letter next to the best answer.

1. Which of these is a **problem** that fingerprints can **solve**?
   A measuring the bones of wanted criminals
   B wanting to change a person's appearance
   C identifying a specific individual
   D needing witnesses with good memories

2. What makes each fingerprint unique?
   A whether they are latent or visible
   B the shape, position, and size of their pattern
   C the surface from which the prints are lifted
   D their placement on an object

3. What is the main idea of this article?
   A The bone measurements of two different people can be identical.
   B There are forensic scientists in crime labs all over the world.
   C Fingerprints were not widely used until the late 1800s.
   D Fingerprinting was a great step forward for forensic science.

Write your answers on the lines.

4. Why can fingerprints be used to verify a person's identity?

____

____

5. What **solutions** did people use to identify people in the past?

____

____

____

6. What development was the beginning of "the age of scientific crime detection"?

____

____

Get Organized

Fill in the chart to show a **solution** to each potential **problem**.

Problem Two people look exactly alike and have the same name.	**Solution**
Problem The police need to look at thousands of fingerprints to find a match.	**Solution**
Problem A fingerprint is left on a table, but it cannot be seen.	**Solution**

Summarize

Suppose that you are a forensic scientist. A reporter asks how to classify fingerprints. Summarize what you know about the way fingerprints are classified.

Write Away!

Team Up

Work with a partner. Observe each other's fingerprints. How are they different? What makes each unique?

My Fingerprints	My Partner's Fingerprints

On Your Own

Fingerprints can be a **problem** if they point to the wrong suspect. Imagine that your fingerprints have been found at a crime scene. Write a statement that explains the way your fingerprints got there and why they do not prove your guilt.

WRITER'S CHECKLIST

- ☐ Write a statement for the police.
- ☐ Describe the reason your fingerprints were found at the crime scene.
- ☐ Explain why they do not prove your guilt.

Evaluating Evidence

Problems and Solutions in Math

Numbers can help make people aware of a **problem**. Numbers can also help people look for the right **solution**, especially when investigators are trying to identify the person who committed a crime. Forensic scientists use evidence to rule out some people as suspects and to prove who is really guilty.

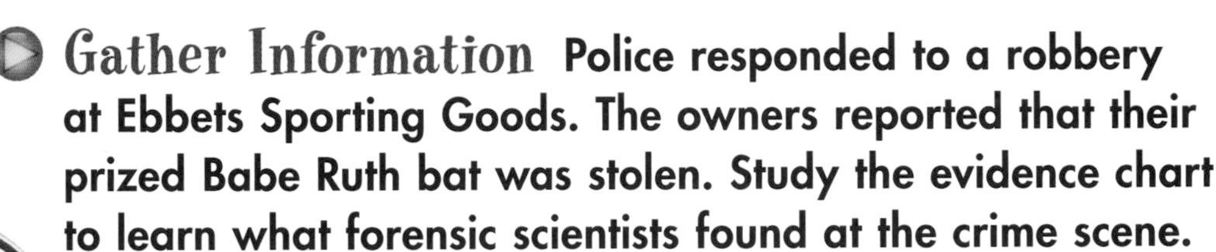

Gather Information **Police responded to a robbery at Ebbets Sporting Goods. The owners reported that their prized Babe Ruth bat was stolen. Study the evidence chart to learn what forensic scientists found at the crime scene.**

Evidence Chart
• Footprint from a size-8 running shoe
• 1 brown hair, 6 inches long
• 1 16-ounce bottle of water, unopened
• 2 smudged fingerprints on the bottle, probably from a right hand
• Shells from 24 peanuts
• 1 New York Yankees baseball cap, size 7
• 1 hamburger wrapper

Use a Suspect Chart

A suspect chart can help investigators solve crimes. They mark evidence that suggests a suspect is guilty with ✔. They mark evidence that suggests a suspect is innocent with ✘. Use the evidence and suspect charts to answer the questions.

Lorenzo	Isabelle
✔ brown hair	✘ blonde hair
✔ right-handed	✘ left-handed
✔ size-8 feet	✘ size-6 feet
✘ hat size 7 1/2	✔ hat size 7
✘ drinks only iced tea	✘ allergic to peanuts

1. What is the **problem** with choosing Isabelle as the guilty suspect?

____

____

2. What keeps you from thinking that Lorenzo is guilty?

____

3. Why was Lorenzo's brown hair not proof of his guilt?

____

Make Your Own Suspect Chart

Fill in the suspect chart below using ✔ and ✘ as above. Decide which of the suspects you think is guilty, and explain the way you reached your solution.

Bridget	Dustin
brown hair	red hair
right-handed	right-handed
size-9 feet	size-8 feet
hat size 7	hat size 7
vegetarian	Babe Ruth fan
Returned from vacation the day after the robbery	lives 2 blocks from Ebbets Sporting Goods

Solution: ____

____

Making Connections

Read the article below. Then answer the questions.

Ancient Mystery Solved

King Tut is one of the most recognizable names in the world. This Egyptian king was most likely only a teenager when he died over 3,000 years ago. Since the discovery of his burial place in 1922, there have been questions about King Tut, especially about the way he died. With the help of forensics, some questions are finally being answered.

In 1968, X-rays were taken of Tut's mummy, which revealed that there were fragments of bone in his skull. At that time, scientists concluded that King Tut had died from an injury to the back of the head. This led some people to believe that the young king had been murdered.

However, the tests were not conclusive, and people still wondered who or what killed King Tut. As new forensic techniques were developed, scientists reopened the case of King Tut's death.

One of the new tests run in 2005 was a CT scan of Tut's body, the first ever performed on an Egyptian mummy. A CT scan is a three-dimensional X-ray image of an object. The scans showed that Tut had suffered a badly broken left thighbone before his death, and it had never healed.

The new evidence showed that Tut probably did not die from a blow to the back of his head. Instead, many scientists now believe that the young king died of an infection caused by his broken leg.

Because of forensic science, people know better than ever before what caused King Tut's death. Still, no one can be completely sure.

1. What was the **problem** that forensic scientists were trying to **solve**?

___

2. What forensic tools did scientists use to **solve** the case of King Tut?

___

3. What other **problems** might forensic scientists **solve** in the case of King Tut?

___

___

Apply Your Knowledge **Think about the story "Mystery on the 13th Floor" and the articles you have read in this unit. Answer the questions below.**

What kind of forensic science would you enjoy? Write a short paragraph describing the type of forensic scientist you might like to be someday.

____

____

____

____

What parts of forensic science might be difficult for you? Explain the ways you might **solve** this **problem**.

____

____

____

____

Choose a Team Project **Choose one of the following group activities, and complete it using your knowledge of forensic science.**

Wrongly Accused

Imagine that a member of your group has been accused of a crime that he or she did not commit. With your group, make a list describing the scene of the crime and the clues that were found there. Then prepare a case that uses evidence and forensic science to prove his or her innocence. Read your defense to the class. Try to convince them as if they were the jury.

Future Forensics

In your group, invent a mystery television program that focuses on forensic science in the year 2050. What kinds of crimes would the characters need to solve, and what new technology might they use? Write a scene from this new thriller. Then act out the scene for your class, with each group member playing the part of one of the main characters.

Acknowledgments

Editorial Director Stephanie Muller
Editor Jen Rassler
Book Coordinator Michele Jester
Design Director Sharon Golden
Content Development Words & Numbers
Design and Production The Format Group, LLC
Vice President of Production and Manufacturing Doreen Smith
Production Manager Jason Grasso
Production Editor Tracy Wilhelmy
Prepress Coordinator Todd Kochakji

Illustration and photography credits:

Cover Artist Jeff Wack

Student Letter p. v © Comstock Images / Alamy

Unit 1 pp. 2, 3, 4 Laura Fernandez; p. 8 Mitsuaki Iwago/Minden Pictures; p. 9 Getty Images; p. 14 © Bettman/Corbis; p. 15 Library of Congress Prints & Photographs Division; p. 16 Robert Weight; Ecoscene/Corbis

Unit 2 pp. 24, 25, 26 Raul Rodriquez Allen; p. 37 Library of Congress Prints & Photographs Division; p. 38 © Michael S. Yamashita/CORBIS; p. 42 Steve Toole; p. 43 Steve Toole

Unit 3 pp. 46, 47, 48 Annabelle Hartmann; p. 52 © Bettmann/CORBIS; p. 52 © Eric and David Hosking/CORBIS; p. 53 © Underwood & Underwood/CORBIS; p. 53 Steve Toole; p. 54 © Bettmann/CORBIS; p. 54 Frank Lane Picture Agency/CORBIS; p. 58 © Alison Wright/CORBIS; p. 59 © James Davis/Eye Ubiqitous/CORBIS; p. 60 © Gideon Mendel/CORBIS; p. 66 Steve Toole

Unit 4 pp. 68, 69, 70 Paul Rivoche; p. 74 © Jim Campbell/Aero-News Network/Pool/Reuters/Corbis; p. 75 © Airbus Industrie/Handout/Reuters/Corbis; p. 76 TOM TSCHIDA/NASA; p. 80 © SCPhotos/Alamy ; p. 81 © The Art Archive/Bibliotheque des Arts Decoratifs Paris/Dagli Orti; p. 82 © Kean Collection/Getty Images; p. 86 Library of Congress Prints & Photographs Division; p. 87 Steve Toole; p. 87 Steve Toole; p. 88 © Tyson V. Rininger

Unit 5 pp. 90, 91, 92 Christopher Burch/Creative Freelancers; p. 96 © Gerry Ellis/Digitalvision/Getty Images; p. 97 Francine Mastrangelo; p. 98 © Gerry Ellis/Digitalvision/Getty Images; p. 102 © Martin Harvey/CORBIS; p. 103 © Frank Lukasseck/zefa/Corbis; p. 104 © Martin Harvey/CORBIS; p. 109 Steve Toole; p. 110 © Digitalvision/Getty Images

Unit 6 pp. 112, 113, 114 Stephen Elford; p. 118 ©David Stoecklein/CORBIS; p. 119 © Christophe Paucellier/Photo & Co./Corbis ; p. 120 Steve Toole; p. 124 Digital Vision/Getty; p. 125 © YOSHIKAZU TSUNO/AFP/Getty Images; p. 126 ©Digital Vision/Getty; p. 130 ©Bob and Carol Keck; p. 131 Steve Toole

Unit 7 pp. 134, 135, 136 Laura Fernandez; p. 140 NOAA George E. Marsh Album; p. 141 Library of Congress, Prints and Photographs Division, FSA-OWI Collection [LC-USF34-018281-C]; p. 142 Library of Congress, Prints and Photographs Division, FSA-OWI Collection [LC-DIG-fsa-8b38341]; p. 146 © Bettmann/CORBIS; p. 147 © CORBIS; p. 148 © Joseph Schwartz/CORBIS; p. 150 Library of Congress, Prints & Photographs Division, FSA/OWI Collection, [LC-USF34-039186-D]; p. 154 Library of Congress Prints & Photographs Division

Unit 8 pp. 156, 157, 158 Scott Goto/Creative Freelancers; p. 162 © brand X Pictures/Alamy; p. 163 © John Chiasson/Liaison/Getty Images; p. 164 © Jim Craigmyle/CORBIS; p. 168 © William Whitehurst/CORBIS; p. 170 © Keith Srakocic/AP Wideworld Photos

NOTES

NOTES